GrowLab

A Complete Guide to Gardening in the Classroom

KidsGardening.org
132 Intervale Rd
Burlington, Vermont 05401

Authors	Eve Pranis, KidsGardening.org
	Jack Hale, Knox Parks Foundation
Editors	Nancy Cornell, Cheryl Dorschner, Sarah Pounders, Barbara Richardson
Design	Lynn Severance, Alison Watt, Andrea Warren
Illustrators	Bruce Conklin, Lynn Severance
Cover Design	Randall Leers
Project Managers	Larry Sommers, Katherine Stahl

Special Technical Note:

This book was written to be used with a GrowLab® Indoor Garden, however the general gardening content presented can apply to any indoor garden including prefabricated or DIY grow light structures and windowsill plantings. If you are using a prefabricated light garden system, make sure to follow any special instructions regarding set up, operations and maintenance provided with your unit.

Many of the designations used by manufacturers and sellers to distinguish their products are claimed as trademarks. Where those designations appear in this book and KidsGardening.org is aware of a trademark claim, the designations have been printed in initial caps.

GrowLab® is a registered trademark of Gardener's Supply Company.

Published by KidsGardening.org.

Copyright © 2016 by KidsGardening.org, 132 Intervale Rd, Burlington, Vermont 05401 and the Knox Parks Foundation, 150 Wallbridge Avenue, West Hartford, Connecticut 06119.

Third Edition, 2018

Library of Congress Control Number: 2018957413

ISBN-13: 978-0-9992234-4-4
ISBN-10: 0-9992234-4-5

Contents

Preface

The foundation for KidsGardening sprouted from the youth gardening work of the National Gardening Association founded in 1972. Through the years, our efforts have provided support for thousands of school and community gardening programs. We've watched children's curiosity blossom and confidence grow as they care for plants. We have listened to their questions as they puzzle out the great mysteries of growth. We have seen them renew their interest in regular school subjects that are enriched by the gardening experience. And we've provided teachers with educational materials and grant resources to help them implement interdisciplinary lessons.

Because not all teachers and youth leaders are lucky enough to have outdoor garden space, adequate time, or a climate that allows for year-round gardening, in 1986, our Education Specialists Eve Pranis and Joy Cohen began to search for an exemplary indoor school gardening program that teachers could easily use indoors, during any season, in any climate. We found a model indoor gardening program developed by the Knox Parks Foundation in Hartford, Connecticut. Launched in 1981, the Knox Parks Foundation program used wooden-framed fluorescent lighting units that allowed children to garden in the classroom all winter. Five years later, the Foundation had placed at least one growing unit in every school in Hartford.

Using this program as a base, Eve and Joy adapted and expanded the Knox Parks model to develop the GrowLab indoor gardening program for national use. The result was The GrowLab: Classroom Activities Guide, a K-8 curriculum guide offering a comprehensive curriculum to explore core science and environmental education topics. The primary objective of GrowLab is to help educators spark students' curiosity about plants and engage them in thinking and acting like scientists.

Realizing that not every teacher wishing to enrich classroom studies with a garden will have a professionally designed GrowLab, this second guide, GrowLab: A Complete Guide to Gardening in the Classroom, was developed to guide educators in any type of indoor gardening experience including other fluorescent light units or windowsill gardens. The goal is to demonstrate for educators how the lessons featured in the GrowLab Activities Guide can be practical for all indoor gardening efforts regardless of the size of the gardening space available.

Seventy-five teachers in classrooms nationwide field-tested a draft of this book, providing extensive feedback based on their own classroom gardening experiences. As a result, this guide provides all the information necessary to successfully integrate gardening into school classrooms: step-by-step planting instructions, tips on seed varieties, plans

"I always visit my plants first thing in the morning, sometimes to water them and other times just to talk to them — it's great — like watching your own children grow up!"

— *sixth grader, Cleveland, Ohio*

for a build-it-yourself GrowLab, instructions for garden maintenance and how to leave your garden over vacation, hints on building support for your program, and innovative ideas for integrating gardening activities into your curriculum. The goal of this guide is to provide all teachers, green thumbs or not, with the information necessary to ensure a thriving indoor classroom gardening program.

We hope this guide will help you begin your youth gardening journey. We also offer a wide range of additional resources including online lesson plans and activities, grant programs and additional guide books to support you in your efforts to use plants and gardens to help young minds grow. You can learn more about our programs and resources on page 107. Please contact us with questions and news of your successes and challenges. We'll make every effort to bring you the products and information you ask for, and to put you in touch with local resource people.

We wish you success in your classroom gardening endeavors. We hope your indoor garden becomes the lively focal point of your "growing" classroom.

Acknowledgements

GrowLab: A Complete Guide to Gardening in the Classroom is based on a school gardening program in Hartford, Connecticut, developed by the Knox Parks Foundation. Special thanks to Suzanne Gerety and the Knox Parks Foundation Board of Directors for their involvement in this cooperative effort. We wish to thank the CIGNA Corporation in Hartford, Connecticut for its support of the Knox Parks Foundation's original indoor gardening program. It was through our shared vision that GrowLab has become a broad-based national program.

We sincerely thank the more than seventy-five teachers in eleven cities who have worked with KidsGardening.org to field-test GrowLab: A Complete Guide to Gardening in the Classroom. Their feedback has helped us to develop a comprehensive classroom gardening guide that is a valuable resource for teachers across the country.

We appreciate the members of the Cleveland School Gardening Committee who shared their thoughts and experiences during the research and writing of this book and assisted in the pilot demonstration of the GrowLab gardening units in Cleveland, Ohio, classrooms in 1986.

Our special thanks to:

The many National Gardening Association members whose dedicated gifts of time, money, and enthusiasm have been a constant inspiration.

The foundations who share our vision of a world where young people value the land and learn to become responsible caretakers of the planet. We especially wish to thank the Wallace Genetic Foundation for ongoing support and the many Cleveland foundations who helped us in the earliest days of this program's development:

Biskind Development Corporation
The Cleveland Foundation
The 1525 Foundation
The George Gund Foundation
Premier Industrial Foundation
The Sears Family Foundation
The Sedwick Fund

We also thank those corporations in the gardening industry who have contributed to the development of the GrowLab Program in their role as NGA Corporate Associates.

For assistance with the GrowLab design, we thank: Donald Jackson, carpentry consultant; Michael Kirick, electrical consultant; and Al Mazzeo, Supervisor, Office of Horticulture, Cleveland Public Schools.

Many thanks to our sharp reviewers, who spent time and sincere effort reading and commenting on the manuscript: Sarah Adams, teacher, Starksboro, Vermont; Anne Browne, Principal, South Burlington, Vermont; Florence Cayeros, retired teacher, New York, New York; Paula Flaherty, Teacher, South Burlington, Vermont; Virginie Fowler Elbert, President, Indoor Gardening Society of America, Inc., New York, New York; Lisa Glick, Co-Director, Life Lab Science Program, Santa Cruz, California; Mary Heins, Teacher, Starksboro, Vermont; Casey Murrow, President, The Teachers' Laboratory, Brattleboro, Vermont; Leonard Perry, Cooperative Extension Horticulturist, University of Vermont, Burlington, Vermont; Debi Eglit Tidd, Coordinator, San Francisco League of Urban Gardeners, San Francisco, California.

Introduction

A teacher who chooses to bring gardening into the classroom offers students a chance to get swept up in the excitement of discovery and accomplishment. Gardening programs encourage students to see themselves as scientists, inquirers — active participants in the learning process.

Through gardening, students witness the miracle of life cycles. They tend plants from seed to fruit and back to seed. They gain an understanding of ecosystems, food origins, and the internal dynamics of plant growth. At the same time, they learn practical horticultural skills that last a lifetime.

The classroom garden also provides a motivating, hands-on context for teaching a wide variety of basic principles in science, math, social studies, language arts, health, and fine arts. It's a dynamic tool for delivering interdisciplinary lessons designed to meet required curriculum standards. The multitude of gardening activities makes it easy to accomplish teaching goals and objectives. Whatever activities you choose — from conducting acid rain experiments to growing a salad feast for the whole class, from measuring and graphing root development to pollinating cucumbers — your gardening program will spark children's natural curiosity about living things, and challenge them to develop critical thinking skills.

A "classroom garden" project can be as simple as a small pot of herbs on a windowsill or as ambitious as planting a half acre of vegetables in the schoolyard. By identifying your needs, defining goals, and assessing resources, you can design a program that is right for you.

Don't let lack of garden experience get in your way. Teachers all over the country confirm that you don't have to have a green thumb to have a thriving classroom garden. As one fifth-grade teacher explains,

> I had never been a gardener, but I decided to start a classroom garden because I felt it would be such a valuable experience for my kids. I was nervous at first because I certainly didn't have all the answers. But my students and I learn together, and I'm thrilled to say that four years later the garden is still going strong. It has become an invaluable teaching tool and is the envy of the hallway.

This book provides the how-to details to help you begin an indoor garden. Although both indoor and outdoor gardens provide opportunities for successful gardening programs, indoor gardens are often easier to implement and maintain. The indoor garden provides opportunities for hands-on activities year round without the concern of weather. This is especially beneficial to schools in areas with long winters. Also, an indoor garden provides constant exposure to your plants, which can increase your students' interest and involvement in their projects. Time is also a factor. Indoor gardens may take less time

"We give life by breathing out carbon dioxide for the plants, and the plants breathe out oxygen for us. It's teamwork. It's awesome. If plants weren't around, we wouldn't be around."

— *fourth grader, Burlington, Vermont*

and smaller blocks of time to maintain (dependent, of course, on the size of the indoor garden). It's easy to spend 10 minutes caring for plants in the classroom, but it may take 5 to 10 minutes just to travel to an outdoor garden.

Because it was designed for school gardeners, a prefabricated or homemade GrowLab Indoor Garden is ideal for classroom use. Its light configuration enables you to grow many vegetables, flowers, and herbs to maturity within a reasonable time. The frame is durable and easy to assemble, and holds enough pots for a full-size classroom garden. Even without a GrowLab, your class can grow crops successfully indoors using a sunny windowsill or one or two fluorescent or LED light fixtures. You can apply the information in this guide to any indoor garden situation.

If you're a beginning gardener, or are unsure just how much gardening you wish to undertake with your students, it's best to start small. Begin with a few pots of various vegetables or flowers, and expand as you and your students develop confidence and expertise.

You may be wondering where to begin and exactly what role the indoor garden will play in your classroom. Whether you use your garden as a life science laboratory or as the thematic focus for lessons in all subject areas throughout the year, **Chapter 1,** Using an Indoor Garden in Your Classroom, will help you plan. It offers an array of teacher-proven suggestions for integrating gardening into your curriculum and includes many activity and experiment ideas. It also describes how to build support for an indoor gardening program within the school and community.

Chapters 2 through 6 tell you all you'll need to know to cultivate a successful garden. Topics include obtaining necessary supplies, planning, planting and tending plants, caring for equipment, managing pest problems, and maintaining your garden. These chapters provide the core information necessary to successfully manage an indoor garden. For those who want extended and additional background information, we've included some sections titled "Digging Deeper." The information in these sidebar sections provides additional insights that will be useful in developing curriculum activities, lessons, and experiments.

The Appendices offer a wide range of useful information, including a comprehensive Indoor Garden Growers' Guide, which may well become your favorite section. It contains charts with specific growing information on every recommended vegetable, flower, and herb, as well as detailed planting and harvesting instructions. The appendices also include special project ideas, complete plans for building your own GrowLab, and reproducible worksheets.

We suggest that you read through the Contents to understand the breadth of information included in the guide. The guide is organized so that it can be an efficient reference. If you are new to gardening indoors, you should read the entire book before embarking on your gardening project.

"The first time I ever heard from some parents was when they began calling to find out about the indoor garden that their children were describing at home."

— third-grade teacher, Hartford, Connecticut

GrowLab: A Complete Guide to Gardening in the Classroom

Below is a key to the symbols you'll find in the text:

Additional background information. These sections will help you develop lessons and activity ideas in addition to those described in Chapter 1.

Highlights of the indoor garden activities developed in the classroom field-test sites across the country.

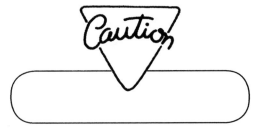

Important safety information.

Helpful additional information. These notes sometimes highlight differences between the pre-fabricated and build-your-own GrowLabs.

"My principal had never visited my classroom in all the time I'd worked at the school. When I set up the garden, he became so intrigued with the whole concept that I offered him a pot, some soil, and a few seeds of his own. Now he comes in almost every day to check on his cucumbers and see what my students are up to."

— *fifth-grade teacher, Hartford, Connecticut*

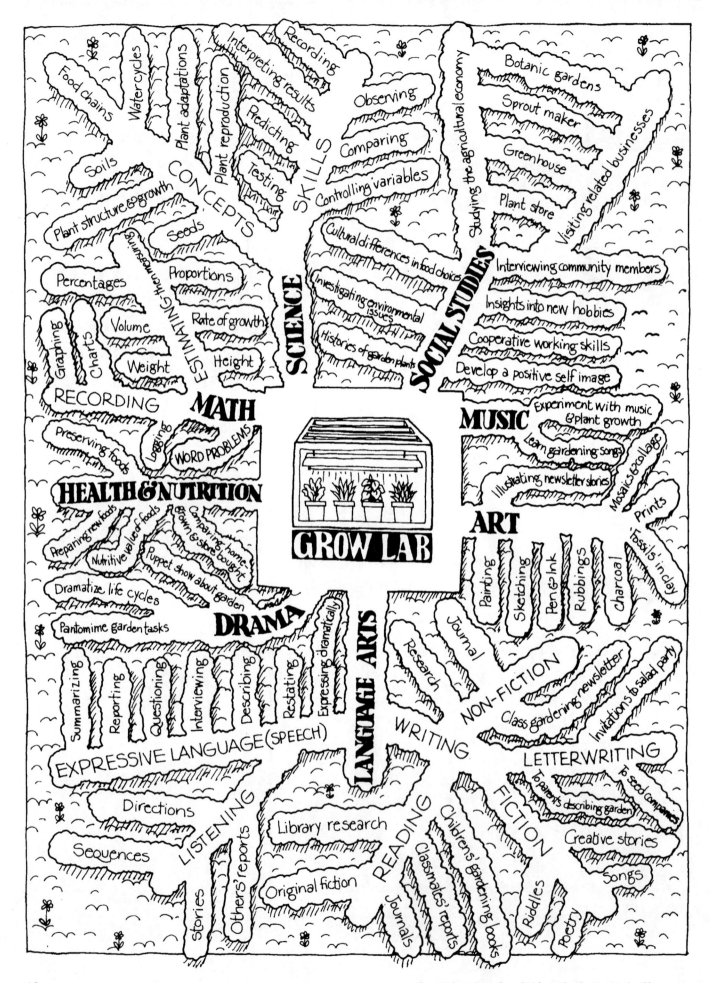

Chapter 1

Using an Indoor Garden in Your Classroom

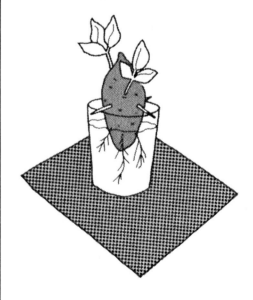

J ust as any gardener needs to consider personal growing preferences in deciding how to manage a garden plot, so each teacher has to decide how indoor gardening best fits his or her own teaching style. Some teachers like to use the garden once a year as an exciting addition to the regular science, math, social studies, or language arts program. Others use the indoor garden as a thematic centerpiece for a yearlong interdisciplinary curriculum. The drawing on the previous page is a visual representation of an interdisciplinary approach to classroom gardening.

This chapter offers many ideas for using the garden to enrich your curriculum in all subject areas. It also describes several exciting thematic classroom garden projects that can provide a culminating activity for the class. The lists that follow represent just a sampling of subject area activities with a gardening focus. Peruse books, magazines, and Web sites for additional ideas. The possibilities are endless!

Science

The process of science is not limited to any one fixed method or approach. Science is a dynamic, multifaceted endeavor. We all use scientific process skills — observing, classifying, inferring, measuring, predicting, organizing and interpreting data, forming hypotheses, and identifying variables — as we explore the world around us.

An indoor garden provides an exciting opportunity for students to hone these scientific process skills. We recommend using the following Garden Experiments for Growing Minds sequence to guide controlled classroom experiments. It uses garden metaphors in place of traditional scientific method steps.

Thinking Like a Scientist

Students in one fifth-grade classroom were curious about the effectiveness of different growing mixes, so they set up this experiment.

1. **Plant a question.** Do tomatoes produce more fruit when the plants are grown in sand, clay, soilless mix, or garden soil?

2. **Sprout a guess.** From what we've learned about soils, we believe that the plants will grow best in the rich garden soil. We're not sure whether the sand or soilless mix will support better growth. Because they are both so light and well drained, we believe the plants will grow equally well in sand and soilless mix. Since clay is so heavy and poorly drained, we predict that the seedlings will grow poorly in it because they will have poor root growth and less oxygen available to them.

3. **Design a growing experiment.** We will fill two 6-inch pots with each of the four growing media. We will plant two three-week-old tomato seedlings in each of the eight pots.

   Control Variables. In order to control the variables, we will put all of the pots in the center of the GrowLab and we'll water each pot with 1 cup of water twice a week. (We won't fertilize any of the plants since we assume that the four mixes have different nutrients available and we want to see how that affects the growth of the plants.)

4. **Record fruitful observations.** We will measure and chart the height of the seedlings every day, taking an average of the height of the seedlings in each pot. We will observe the color of the leaves, number of leaves, and, eventually, the number of flowers and weight of fruit. When the plants have matured, we will pull them up and examine their root systems, making an estimate of total root length. We will record our observations.

5. **Harvest conclusions.** We will use the records of our observations to describe how the tomato plants grew in each of the four growing mixes. We will base our final conclusion on the total weight of fruit produced in each pot.

Garden Experiments for Growing Minds

1. **Plant a question.** Children are naturally curious about their environment. Their imaginative musings and questions can become the basis for scientific investigations. As students observe and explore their indoor garden, constantly encourage questions. Help students identify questions that can lead to a garden experiment.

2. **Sprout a guess.** Encourage students to make educated guesses to answer their questions, predicting the outcome of their experiment.

3. **Design a growing experiment.** Decide together which crops you'll use and how you'll set up your experiment. When planning experiments that include growing plants, consider quick-maturing crops such as radishes or lettuce. Experiments with these crops can be done almost any time, while experiments with slower-growing crops like tomatoes need to be started early. Beans are a good crop to use for studying full life cycles. Corn is ideal for experiments testing growth rates in response to different variables, but it's too tall to be grown to maturity under lights.

   Use the Grower's Guide (Appendix A) to determine planting times, so important steps in the experiment won't coincide with a school vacation.

   Control variables. Arranging for all but the experimental variable to remain constant is an important part of any scientific experiment. In the classroom garden you can keep heat and light relatively constant. If you are keeping light constant, be sure to rotate plants occasionally to ensure that all plants receive equal exposure. (See page 44 for more on light.) There will also be differences in temperature and humidity between the edges of the GrowLab and the middle. Water and fertilizer are other variables you and your students can control.

   To ensure a big enough sample for drawing conclusions, plant at least two containers of each type of seed or plant for each treatment. This repetition will increase confidence in your experimental conclusions.

4. **Record fruitful observations.** Observing and recording data are both essential parts of the scientific process and important gardening practices. Below is a list of the types of observations you and your students can make during experiments:

   Measure and weigh the plants (fruit, foliage, roots) at predetermined intervals or at the end of the experiment. Graph the results.

   Measure and count fruits and flowers.

   Describe, compare, and contrast the appearance of plant parts as seen with and without a microscope.

   Describe, compare, and contrast the taste of edible plant parts and fruits.

   Describe observations with narratives, graphs, charts, drawings, and photographs.

5. **Harvest conclusions.** Students can summarize results and draw conclusions in written and/or oral form. If conclusions contradict conventional scientific wisdom (e.g., students find that plants grow

better in the dark than in the light!), have students generate ideas to explain what they think led to their unusual results.

Once students have drawn conclusions, they can apply new information to other situations and make fresh predictions. Your science experiments will hopefully stimulate more questions and lead to further investigations, and the cycle will begin again. So, plant a question and watch it grow!

Below you'll find a few ideas for plant, physical, and earth science activities in the classroom garden. Those marked with ❧ are appropriate for controlled classroom experiments.

Visit KidsGardening.org for additional classroom activity and lesson ideas.

Plant Science

What are the differences between living and nonliving things? How are humans like plants? How are they different? Distinguish and describe differences and similarities.

What are the similarities and differences among seeds? Sort and classify seeds according to their characteristics.

How do seeds work? Observe and identify the functions of seed parts.

❧ Do vegetable seeds germinate better in light or dark? At what depth do they germinate most quickly? At what temperature do they germinate most quickly?

How does a plant grow? Investigate the functions of different plant structures (cotyledons, roots, stems, leaves, flowers, fruits).

What do plants need to grow? Do all plants need the same things? Study the various conditions different plants need to grow.

❧ How does crowding affect the growth and quality of plants?

Will vegetable plants grow differently in clay, sand, garden soil, and potting mix? Experiment by growing a control plant in each.

How do roots grow? Plant a seed against the side of a clear glass or plastic container and observe root growth.

❧ Will plants grow faster if they are fertilized every day?

❧ Do plants really grow toward light?

❧ Do shoots always grow up and roots always grow down?

❧ What would happen if we watered our plants with tea, soft drinks, etc.?

How do plants reproduce? Dissect flowers. Pollinate cucumbers. Start plants from cuttings, bulbs, tubers, spores.

❧ Do plants need light to photosynthesize? Try using black paper to block the light from some leaves for a period of time. Use iodine to test whether the lack of light prevents starch production.

❧ Could plants live without CO_2 entering through the leaves? Cover some plant leaves with petroleum jelly to test this question.

What is the life cycle of a flowering plant? Observe and record the stages of the life cycle from seed to fruit to seed.

❧ Do plants respond to different durations of light? Use your timer to investigate this.

Earth and Physical Science

What is the water cycle? How does it work? Simulate the water cycle in the indoor garden by covering it with a "dome" of clear plastic. Study and observe the transpiration, evaporation, and condensation of water.

How are some soils different from others? Compare and contrast the properties of different types of soils (density, air spaces, living organisms, composition, texture, smell, appearance).

How do different plants respond to different climates? Create different climates in your indoor garden and observe plant growth.

❧ What is pH? How does it affect plants? Use litmus paper or test kits to test the pH of different soils. Investigate how plants respond to soils with different pH levels.

❧ How might acid rain affect the growth of plants? Water plants with solutions of different pH and observe differences in plant growth.

❧ What are the properties of different types of light? Cover pots with cellophane of different colors to screen out all but one wavelength of light from plants. Observe plant growth.

How does energy change to matter during photosynthesis?

How does water change from a liquid to a gas state in the indoor garden?

Environmental Science

Investigate food chains and webs.

Simulate soil erosion in your classroom garden. Observe the difference in soil loss when water is splashed on a tilted planted pot, and on a tilted unplanted pot.

Compare and contrast outside ecosystems with your indoor garden ecosystem. How are they similar and how are they different?

❧ Conduct an experiment to simulate the effects of road salt on plant growth. Water plants with salt solutions of various strengths and observe differences in plant growth.

Research the accumulation of harmful substances in the food chain.

Discuss the concept of seed diversity. Try saving some of your own seeds to plant again.

Observe and compare wild plants and cultivated plants.

Cotton, Deserts, Rain Forests

CLASSROOM PROFILE

One third-grade teacher complemented part of his social studies curriculum by growing cotton in a GrowLab. With some skepticism, his class planted the seeds to enhance a unit on Black history. Nine months later, much to the surprise and delight of the students and teacher, they harvested thirty cotton bolls from four plants. The students have saved the seeds and next year they plan to try cleaning and spinning some of their harvest!

The same teacher incorporated his GrowLab into a study of climates. Since this class had two indoor gardens, students were able to simulate a desert climate in one and a tropical climate in the other. The desert climate GrowLab was kept very dry and housed cacti and other desert-type plants. The tropical GrowLab housed many houseplants of tropical origin. It was kept enclosed in a plastic tent, the base material was kept constantly moist, and plants were misted twice a week.

The students speculated about how plants would grow in their respective suitable climates and made careful observations. As a final project, the students developed some questions (e.g., What would happen if we tried to grow cactus in a tropical climate?). They hypothesized about likely results and then observed and recorded what actually happened when they tried it.

Incorporating Other Subjects

In addition to its role as a science laboratory, your classroom garden can act as a springboard for lessons in math, social studies, language arts, health and nutrition, music, drama, and art. For example, the laboratory for plant science experiments can also serve as a salad garden. While studying the water cycle or measuring and charting plant growth rates, students can also raise plants for holiday gifts, keep garden journals, research the histories of different food plants, write "garden mysteries," and more.

Math

Calculate the number of hours the timer should be on and off. How many hours a week or month will it be on?

Measure and graph the growth rates of plants and make predictions regarding future growth. Use standard and metric measurements.

Keep records of size comparisons and use bar graphs to illustrate.

Predict dates of germination and maturity based on information from seed catalogs.

Plan backwards from salad party or other harvest date to determine when each crop should be planted.

Estimate the number of 6-inch pots that could fit into your indoor garden.

Measure part of a root and estimate the length of the entire root system on a plant. Lay pieces end to end and measure.

Use graph paper to make a map to scale of the area of your garden.

Calculate amounts of fertilizer to use per quart and per liter of water.

Chart temperatures of the air and soil in your garden in Fahrenheit and centigrade.

Determine the weight and volume of soil mix when wet and dry.

Compare prices of produce in markets to determine the value of your garden produce.

Count the total number of flower buds, and the number of buds that actually produce fruit. Figure a percentage or fraction of the total that fruited.

Project the amount of profit that can be made from a plant sale and plan accordingly.

History and Social Studies

Research and report on cultural/ethnic differences in food consumption and gardening practices.

To enhance a study of economic crops, try growing cotton, corn, soybeans, or wheat. (Note: most cannot be grown to maturity indoors.)

Research local agricultural history.

Fundraising with Seedlings

Some classes use their gardening skills for entrepreneurial ventures. One ambitious sixth-grade gardening classroom decided to raise enough seedlings and houseplant cuttings to help finance a class trip. Students planned and projected income based on the fact that their single 8-square-foot GrowLab could hold more than 100 school milk cartons, or three dozen 5-by-7-inch market packs.

In the fall, students started houseplant cuttings, marigolds, and herbs for gift plants, and sold them at a holiday plant sale. After winter vacation, they started garden seeds for a spring seedling sale.

As part of this project, the students studied seed catalogs and other references, then wrote and designed information sheets to go with each plant. They projected income, planned and handled the sales, offered advice to others, and learned some valuable gardening skills. The added bonus of the $200 income helped finance an exciting class field trip from New Jersey to Washington, D.C.

Interview local gardeners and find out what makes them choose to garden (pleasure, economics, health, etc.).

Visit local farms and interview farmers about choosing crops, growing practices, marketing, and the history of their farm.

Collect newspaper or magazine clippings and discuss how advertising influences our food choices.

Discuss how the mingling of cultures has influenced cuisines throughout history, and how it continues to do so in your own community.

Research the histories of classroom garden plants. Discover where they originated, the impact they've had on our diets, and how today's varieties differ from the original plants.

Study some of the political, ecological, and economic reasons for hunger and what can be done locally and globally to eradicate it.

Use the classroom garden to complement a study of the influence of climate on food production.

Language Arts

Write, illustrate, and publish a collection of garden stories and poems.

After careful observation, brainstorm adjectives to describe each plant in your garden.

Study new vocabulary that relates to plants and gardens.

Write letters to local merchants describing your gardening project and asking for donations of supplies.

Brainstorm a list of questions about the garden the class would like to answer through library or Internet research.

Write a letter to parents describing the indoor garden.

Publish a class newsletter about the garden and distribute it to other classrooms.

Read daily newspapers and magazines and bring in articles that relate to gardening, agriculture, hunger, nutrition, etc.

Write letters to your region's Cooperative Extension Service or garden club to ask for advice and invite guest speakers.

Write creative stories in the first person from the point of view of a particular plant in the indoor garden.

Use the library and Internet to research information about particular plants. Where did they originate? How are they used? Do they require special care? When will they be ready for harvest? Prepare a written or oral report.

Put together a class book with gardening information and advice.

Learn to use seed catalogs.

Write a script and produce a play or puppet show about plants and gardens.

Read and discuss a children's book that relates to plants with the class.

Choose your favorite garden vegetable. List its strong points, then write a script for a sixty-second advertisement designed to get more people to grow and eat it!

Health and Nutrition

Compare the importance of nutrients in the health of humans and of plants.

Study the nutritive value of the various crops in your garden.

Determine from which parts of the plants various foods come. Discuss the difference in nutritional value of various plant parts.

Study adaptations of plant parts that make them good food sources.

Sprout various seeds for eating.

Prepare vegetables in exciting new ways.

Conduct a blindfolded taste test using classroom vegetables and super-market vegetables.

Experiment with food preservation techniques such as drying, freezing, and canning.

Art, Music, and Drama

Create paintings and drawings of garden plants.

Paint a class garden mural to hang in the hallway.

Design labels to mark pots and flats.

Make a seed mosaic, or a food or garden collage.

Make prints from various plant parts.

Make puppets, then write and present a play about garden life, eco-systems, food concerns, etc.

Dramatize the life cycles of garden vegetables.

Pantomime various gardening tasks (transplanting, fertilizing, sowing seeds, pollinating).

Learn songs that relate to food, gardens, and the environment.

Listen to the music of composers inspired by nature.

Experiment with the effects of music on plant growth, health, and behavior.

Design invitations and a menu for a salad party.

Design flyers for a seedling or potted plant sale.

Build clay or tissue paper models of flowers.

Make plant fossils in clay.

Thematic Gardens

If our long list of plant-based curricular activities seems overwhelming, consider using a theme to identify parameters for choosing garden activities. Theme gardens can help you achieve an educational impact in a more organized learning structure, and many thematic projects lend themselves to a culminating special event (i.e. salad party, special-occasion gifts, seedling sale, etc.).

The Food Garden

You can grow vegetables, herbs, and fruits to be harvested and tasted throughout the year, or you can time the planting of your crops to produce a single harvest feast. Producing a tasty garden salad for the whole class is a popular culminating activity that generates excitement and group pride in a job well done. Planning a garden for a particular harvest date requires that you plant crops at different times, since crops mature at different rates. To calculate when to plant each crop, have your students consult the Grower's Guide (Appendix A) for information on days to maturity and count back from the desired date of harvest. The Grower's Guide includes yield and harvest information for each vegetable.

Table 1 provides a sample schedule for a salad garden for a class of thirty, assuming that you're aiming for a May 15-June 1 harvest date.

Your students will be eating much of what they grow in the indoor garden, but remind them that not all plants are edible. Allow them to eat only those plants or plant parts you know to be safe. Alert them to the dangers of eating unknown plant material.

Salad Garden Planning Guide   Table 1

Crop	Planting Date	# 6-Inch Pots	Plants Per Pot
Tomatoes	February 15	2-4	1-2
Basil	March 15	1	4
Parsley	March 15	1	2-3
Lettuce	March 15	8	4
Beans	March 15	1	2
Carrots	March 15	2	6
Beets (for greens)	March 15	2	3
Cucumbers	March 15	1	1
Radishes	April 10	3	4-6
Sprouts	May 10	see sidebar, p. 21	

note:

If plants go home during freezing weather, you must protect them. A paper bag folded and stapled shut usually provides good protection. A leakproof plastic bag inflated and sealed with a knot or a twist tie also works well.

The Gift Plant Garden

Many gardening teachers like to have each child grow a pot of flowers, herbs, vegetables, or a houseplant to take home, often for holidays. Flowers for Mother's Day, such as zinnias or marigolds, are always a big hit.

To choose plants to grow and send home, consult the Growers' Guide (Appendix A) and/or seed packets to determine how far in advance you should sow the seeds. Give the plants an extra week or two of growing time to make sure they each have at least one blossom when its time to send them home.

You can grow gift plants in small containers such as school milk cartons (make a drainage hole in each container with a sharp pencil) or in plastic pots. Students will need to transplant their gifts into larger containers when they get home.

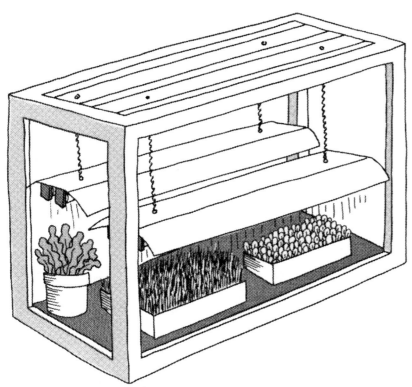

The Seedling Garden

The indoor garden is perfect for starting vegetables, herbs, or flowers that will eventually find their way into a garden or landscape at home or at school. Classes have raised seedlings indoors for many uses including:

> school beautification (planting around flagpole, in borders, or around trees)
>
> class or school gardens
>
> community or food bank gardens
>
> nursing home gardens
>
> seedling sales

It's common for classes to start seeds in milk cartons or in more traditional seed starting containers, such as plastic market packs. Have

DIGGING DEEPER

Topping It Off With Sprouts

Sprouting seeds to top off your garden salad can be a tasty as well as an educational experience. Sprouted seeds enhance the salad's nutritional value by increasing the amount of protein, minerals, and vitamins it provides.

Some questions for investigation during the sprouting activity might include the following: What is a sprout? What do the seeds need to sprout? Can we identify different parts of the plant in a sprout? Why are they so nutritious? When do they turn green?

Although you can sprout many types of seeds for eating, it's best to start with mung beans or alfalfa seeds. Other good sprouting seeds include buckwheat, kidney beans, radishes, and clover. Buy seeds that have been specifically designated for sprouting to ensure they have not been treated with fungicides. These untreated seeds are available in health food stores, in some supermarkets, and through many seed catalogs.

To Sprout Seeds:

1. Soak 2 tablespoons of alfalfa seeds or 5 tablespoons of mung bean seeds overnight in water. Drain and place seeds in a quart jar. Cover the jar with cheesecloth, secured with a rubber band.

2. Place the jar on its side (or tipped slightly downward for better drainage) in a warm (not hot), dim or dark place. Twice a day, rinse seeds with cool tap water and make sure to drain them well through the cheesecloth before replacing the jar on its side.

3. After several days, place the jar in the light for a day or two to encourage green color (as photosynthesis begins) and vitamin production.

4. Enjoy them with your salad!

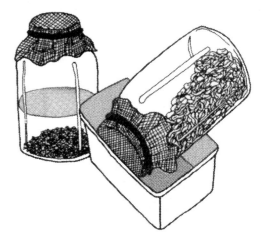

your students consult garden books, seed catalogs, seed packets, and local resources (nurseries and the Cooperative Extension Service, for example) to determine the best times to transplant specific crops outdoors for your area. This will help you plan your indoor planting schedule. Determine your area's last spring frost date, have children count back the number of weeks indicated for each crop, and start seeds accordingly.

Not all crops transplant well. For example, peas and squash have tender root systems and may be shocked from transplanting. Root crops develop small, misshapen, hairy roots if transplanted. Table 2 shows which crops are suitable for transplanting.

Seedling Garden Planning Guide — Table 2

Crop* Outdoors	Number of Weeks from Seedling to Transplanting
Broccoli	5-7 weeks
Cauliflower	5-7
Cabbage	5-7
Celery	10-12
Eggplant	6-8
Leeks	8-10
Lettuce	3-6
Onions	6-8
Parsley	6-8
Peppers	6-8
Tomatoes	6-8

*All annual flowers and herbs listed in the Growers' Guide are suitable for transplanting. Check seed packets to determine when to sow and transplant.

DIGGING DEEPER

Hardening Off Seedlings

If you've raised seedlings to be transplanted outside, you'll need to help them become accustomed to outdoor conditions so they'll survive the change in environments. This process is called hardening off. The best way to harden off plants is to place them outdoors in a cold frame — an unheated enclosure with a removable cover. You can make a temporary cold frame by placing a storm window or door over hay bales arranged to form walls. During the day, raise or remove the cover completely, as long as temperatures stay above freezing. Replace the cover at night. After about two weeks, the seedlings can safely be exposed to the outdoors and planted. If you have neither the space nor the materials for a cold frame, you can harden off seedlings by placing them outside in a partially sheltered spot for progressively longer periods each day, bringing them indoors at night.

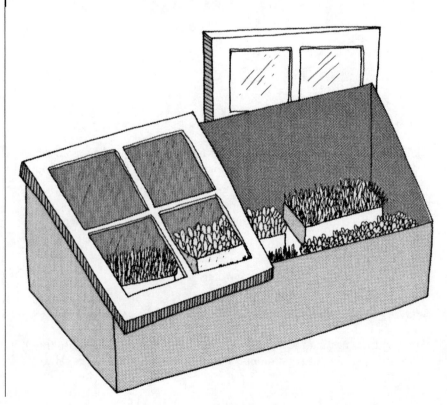

GrowLab: A Complete Guide to Gardening in the Classroom

More Thematic Ideas

There are any number of ways to include an indoor garden in your school curriculum. Students enjoy brainstorming ideas, so be sure to invite their input. Additional ideas include a rainforest garden (grow and learn about rainforest plants), a rainbow garden (grow plants in the colors of the rainbow), an herb garden (grow herbs and make pot-pourri or sachets), and a zoo garden (grow plants with animal names like Lamb's Ear and Kangaroo Paws).

Classroom Gardening and Social Skills

Gardening provides a unique opportunity for promoting personal growth and for demonstrating the value of responsibility, cooperation, and group problem solving. One fifth-grade teacher reported that several of her tough, apathetic students became exuberant, responsible caretakers of their precious plants. Others have noted that withdrawn or disabled students have become intrigued with the classroom garden and felt proud of their accomplishment as their plants thrived. In most cases, children develop respect for the class effort and for the living things they've so carefully tended.

Collaboration and Teamwork

In a seventh-grade classroom, students wondered, How do various soils affect the growth of lettuce? The class developed hypotheses, then divided into groups. Each group tested one hypothesis. They later collaborated on developing conclusions. Then the students discussed how the contribution of each individual had strengthened the cooperative efforts of the whole class, and they noted the value of collaboration in solving complex problems.

One approach to organizing an indoor gardening project is to set up "Expert Teams" — small groups of children who become responsible for a particular aspect of gardening, i.e., fertilizer, light, water, heat and humidity. Each team researches its particular area and becomes the resource for the rest of the class on that topic.

Teachers often wonder whether it's best to have each child take responsibility for planting and caring for one pot, or to have a more communal project, with everyone working to care for all of the plants and sharing in the final harvest party or plant sale.

Communal planting and caretaking may reduce the likelihood that one child will be greatly disappointed by a crop failure in one pot. On the other hand, the potential for a boost in individual pride and self-confidence as students care for their own plants is so great, that you may choose to take that risk. Most teachers find that it makes sense to combine both approaches during the year. In any case, try to make sure there are a few healthy replacement plants available.

In general, the more you involve children in all aspects of the gardening process — setting up the garden, designing and implementing experiments, questioning and initiating investigations — the greater the potential for positive social growth.

DIGGING DEEPER

Building Support

Beyond sparking students' enthusiasm for learning, an indoor garden program can also help you achieve other goals, such as interaction among classrooms, parental and community involvement, and developing a base of volunteers and material support for ensuring the success and sustainability of your growing project.

Gain support within the school. Inform your supervisors, faculty, and staff about your plans and goals for weaving the garden into the curriculum and using it as a hands-on interdisciplinary teaching tool. Invite them to stop in and watch the garden's progress and students' enthusiasm. It's very important to involve custodians — they may be able to help by looking after your garden during school vacations.

Involve parents. It's well known that students perform better when their parents are aware of and attentive to what their children are doing in school. Kids can tell their parents about the indoor garden by writing letters, publishing a classroom newsletter, or inviting them to an open house. It's also an opportunity for garden-savvy parents to contribute their knowledge and skills as classroom aides, guest speakers, or by authoring an article about the indoor garden for a local newspaper.

Inform the community. Children's gardens attract interest from the community, whether from neighbors who can volunteer their gardening knowledge and experience or local businesses seeking a community service partner. Students can invite members of local garden clubs, staff from botanical gardens, Cooperative Extension Service Master Gardeners, garden center and nursery owners, and high school or college service organizations to visit and learn about the garden project. Think of ways these people may be able to help you reach learning goals and invite their involvement in specific ways (e.g., speaking to the class, donating potting soil or fertilizer).

If your school has the desire and opportunity to expand the indoor garden to other classrooms or to the outdoors, you will have a group of people familiar with your program whose support and guidance you can tap into.

Chapter 2

Setting Up Your Indoor Garden

No matter what kind of indoor garden you're using, you'll need to decide on the best location in your room and what kind of base material and covering to use. You'll need to decide what kind of growing mix, containers, and light bulbs to buy, and whether to purchase or build your own indoor light garden or organize a small windowsill garden.

Before you set up your indoor garden, be sure to discuss your gardening project with the school custodian to address concerns he or she may have about the safety or convenience of your new endeavor. Explain the program and the operation of the equipment, and ask the custodian's advice about where to place your classroom garden so that it will not be an inconvenience during routine cleaning. You may also want advice on how to avoid messes, where to discard used soil, how to replace light tubes, and so on.

GrowLab: A Complete Guide to Gardening in the Classroom

Types of Indoor Gardens

Prefabricated GrowLab Indoor Light Gardens and Grow Lights. Pre-fabricated GrowLab Light Gardens and other models of grow light structures are available from numerous commercial sources. Models range from tabletop designs with a single tier of lights to two- and three-tier floor-standing models. They are even available on wheels so they can be moved between multiple classrooms.

Build-it-Yourself GrowLab. Appendix D contains plans for building your own GrowLab. The construction plans were reviewed by licensed electricians and expert carpenters. This unit is known to be safe, sturdy, and effective. It provides similar growing conditions to the traditional one-tier prefabricated model and is an excellent tool for a small indoor garden. While less expensive than a prefabricated GrowLab, construction requires time, tools, and basic carpentry and electrical skills.

Windowsill Garden. If your classroom has windows that receive some sunlight, consider the windowsill option. The amount of light your plants will receive depends on the direction the window faces, the season, whether the sun is blocked by trees or a building, the number of cloudy days in your region, and shade from the roof overhang. Spend a few days monitoring the window to determine the amount of light available. A windowsill garden is obviously the most economical indoor garden option, though it limits the size of your garden and the type of plant you can grow, and provides the least flexibility regarding location.

note:

Prefabricated GrowLabs come with complete instructions for setting up the frame, the electrical components, and the covering. You can also purchase a GrowLab supply kit containing recommended seeds, containers, labels, growing mix, and fertilizer.

Finding the Right Location

Windowsill Gardens. The location of a windowsill garden is restricted by the location of windows in your classroom. Window orientation also has an impact on the amount and quality of light plants will receive. If you have multiple windows to choose from, consider these general guidelines:

Eastern windows receive two to four hours of morning sun. Reserve these locations for growing radishes, lettuce and other leafy vegetables, root vegetables, and houseplants that require minimal light.

Southern windows receive full sun during most of the day and are the best choice for growing most edible crops. Monitor plants closely to make sure tender seedlings and leaves don't get scorched and that soil doesn't dry out.

Western windows generally receive good light exposure for about eight hours a day.

Northern windows receive only diffused light. Most vegetables won't grow well with this exposure, but a number of houseplants will.

GrowLabs. A GrowLab can be placed anywhere in your classroom. The main consideration is the proximity to an electrical outlet and the safety of the electrical cord. Some teachers prefer to position the GrowLab so that students can explore plants from all sides. Others place it against the wall where it takes up less space. Don't place your garden too near a heat source, as this could dry out your plants.

Place a single-tier GrowLab on a sturdy table or counter at your students' eye level. The table should be strong enough to hold at least 100 pounds.

You might think that placing your GrowLab near a window would offer supplementary sunlight, but a GrowLab's light system is specially designed to provide all the light plants normally need. Additional sunlight doesn't hurt, but if a window location subjects your plants to extremes of heat and cold, they will suffer.

Materials and Supplies for Your Garden

The materials and supplies for your indoor garden will vary depending on the option you choose and the plants you grow. The prefabricated and build-it-yourself GrowLabs include additional components: base, base material, light bulbs, and an optional plastic cover. Other necessary supplies include plant containers, growing media, fertilizer, labels, and plants or seeds. A windowsill garden requires a base to protect the windowsill and the same basic supplies.

Indoor Garden Base and Base Material

Your indoor garden needs a base that will catch and hold moisture draining from pots so that it doesn't spill on other surfaces. Prefabricated GrowLab and grow light units usually include heavy-duty plastic trays. For windowsill gardens, use individual plant saucers or narrow trays. Or, create trays out of corrugated cardboard and line them with 6-mil plastic.

We recommend adding a base material — such as moisture grids, perlite, or capillary matting — to trays for best results. Base materials act as a reservoir to supply water and help maintain proper humidity for your plants. They also help to keep soil moist on weekends and during vacations. (See page 48 for more on humidity and page 54 for more on vacation care). Even windowsill plants benefit from the presence of a base material (described below). If you decide to use one, you'll need plastic trays at least 2 inches deep. The following comparison will help you decide which base material is best for you.

Comparing Indoor Garden Base Materials

Moisture Grids — These three-dimensional plastic grids fit inside your plant trays.

Advantages: They are easy to clean, long lasting, and hold enough water for up to a week. Plant roots don't break when you remove pots from the moisture grid. You can add fertilizer to the water so plants can absorb nutrients through their roots.

Disadvantages: Plants can become saturated if you add too much water to trays.

To use grids, insert them in trays, fill trays with water up to the top of the grids, and place plant pots on top. Pots remain above the water

*note:*

You can purchase many indoor gardening supplies from Gardener's Supply Company, and they generously offer a 25% discount to schools and educational institutions. Tell them you heard about the discount from this KidsGardening publication!

level so soil doesn't become waterlogged, yet roots can extend through the grids to absorb moisture. Add more water to trays when the soil surface appears dry.

Perlite

Perlite is volcanic rock that has been expanded into a light-weight, white material by exposure to very high temperatures. It is a common ingredient in potting mixes. You can purchase coarse perlite economically from a greenhouse supply company or a large garden center.

Advantages: Perlite provides good drainage if you overwater plants, it's lightweight, and it reflects light back onto plants. Plant roots can expand into the perilte, and they won't break when you lift pots from the base.

Disadvantages: Perlite is dusty, and the dust can irritate your lungs. To avoid dust, dampen perlite in the bag before pouring it into your garden trays. It's hard to clean perlite when green algae or mold forms, so you'll probably have to replace it once a year.

To use perlite, pour 1 to 1 1/2 inches (approximately 1 cubic foot) of moist perlite in the plastic tray or plastic-lined base. Add 2 to 3 gallons of water. Be sure the material is similarly moist when you leave for the weekend or vacations.

Capillary Matting

This is a nonwoven fabric that acts as a wick. When you place it under potted plants and dip one end into a reservoir of water (e.g., plastic dishpan or pot), it wicks water and provides a continuous supply of moisture for plants.

Advantages: It's easy to set up, relatively easy to clean, doesn't create a mess, can be reused, and is lightweight.

Disadvantages: Using capillary matting makes it somewhat more difficult to maintain adequate moisture during a long vacation. Plant roots sometimes grow into mats and break when you remove pots (lift them every few days to avoid this). The matting loses some absorbency each time you wash it.

If you choose to use capillary matting, there are two ways to set it up:

If you have plastic growers' trays or other 2- to 3-inch deep trays as water reservoirs, lay a rigid piece of plastic, plexiglass, or foam over each tray, and cover it with moistened capillary matting (see figure A). Allow the capillary matting to dip into the tray so several inches can

Perlite dust can irritate respiratory passages. To prevent dust from rising when you pour perlite, moisten it in the bag before pouring it into the base. Cover your nose and mouth with a dust mask or cloth whenever you pour perlite.

figure A

figure B

The special design of the light fixtures in prefabricated GrowLab units allows for ade-quate light with fewer fluorescent tubes than indicated for the build-it-yourself model.

be submerged in water. Fill the trays with water. Using this method, you should be able to maintain adequate moisture reserves for a week or so.

If you don't have plastic trays, lay the matting directly on the plastic in the base of your indoor garden and cut out a "wick" to draw water from a reservoir onto the mat (see figure B, page 27). The wick should be 4 inches wide and 10 inches long. Moisten the matting and the wick and place one end of the wick in the reservoir and one end under the matting. The wick must be firmly in contact with the matting. Although this system will work nicely for maintaining adequate water over long weekends, it's difficult to provide enough water in this way to last more than a week.

Fluorescent and LED Tubes

Prefabricated GrowLabs require two to six tubes depending on the size and model. The Build-it-yourself GrowLab detailed in Appendix D is designed to accommodate six tubes (two tubes in each of three fixtures) suspended over an 8-square-foot base. These setups provide adequate light for growing all classroom garden plants.

You can purchase various types of fluorescent and LED tubes. Different tubes emit different colored light rays (light rays vary by wavelength and are visible as a spectrum of colors from red to blue/violet). Cool white fluorescent tubes — the same as those used for room lighting in most schools — provide light rays from the blue/violent end of the spectrum. They provide sufficient light to grow plants indoors and are the least expensive tubes, but you will probably have to replace them annually since their light intensity decreases with use. A mixture of cool white and warm white fluorescents provides a somewhat better quality of light for overall plant growth (warm lights give off light rays from the red end of the spectrum). Wide-spectrum and full-spectrum fluorescent light tubes provide light rays from col-ors across the spectrum, similar to sunlight. They generally produce better growth, particularly as plants flower and set fruit. These tubes are more expensive, but are generally rated to provide good light intensity for up to three years. Similarly, full-spectrum LED light tubes also meet plants' needs well and although they are more expensive, they provide additional benefits over fluorescent bulbs. LED tubes give off very little heat, they use half the electricity, last longer, are mercury-free, and won't shatter like glass.

If you are gardening on a windowsill, or have only one light fixture, you will not have the light intensity required to bring some indoor crops to maturity, and all crops will take longer to grow. While sin-gle, two-tube fixtures are fine for raising many houseplants with low-light needs, such as African violets or ferns, or for starting seedlings, most vegetable and flower crops need more light to flower and set fruit. The Growers' Guide (Appendix A) indicates which crops are most appropriate for lower light levels.

Covering the Indoor Garden

In most areas of the country, air conditioning and heating systems cause much drier indoor settings than conditions found outdoors. The lack of humidity in the air is a challenge for many plants. It causes them to loose moisture quickly, increasing the water demands of your indoor garden. Although a covering is not absolutely necessary for growing plants, it will help maintain a comfortable humidity and adequate moisture (particularly during vacations) in your garden.

To create a more humid environment for plants, cover your GrowLab on the top and three sides with a polyethylene tent. Many of the pre-fabricated GrowLab models come with a clear plastic climate control tent. For other models or build-it-yourself units, you can purchase a tent or make one from 4- or 6-mil clear polyethylene. Polyethylene in 4-foot widths is available at many discount and hardware stores. Greenhouse supply catalogs also carry this plastic in very large quantities. Avoid lighter-weight plastic because it tears easily.

Cover front only during vacations

On the side of the unit where electrical components are mounted, be sure to attach the plastic **inside** the frame. The electrical components should not be contained within the "tent," since the high humidity can cause the ground fault circuit interrupter to trip unnecessarily. Never lay a covering directly over light fixtures.

Before purchasing or making a cover, check with your custodian regarding local regulations, since some school districts do not allow use of these materials in the classrooms. If you are not allowed to use a plastic covering, you can also use heavy-duty aluminum foil or Mylar, which will increase the amount of light available to your plants, but will limit viewing.

Prefabricated tents slip easily over GrowLabs. If you make your own cover, attach the plastic to the edges of the frame, as illustrated on page 29, with tacks, staples, or duct tape. You can remove the cover or just lift the front panel for better access and viewing, or to increase air circulation as needed. If your garden remains very wet or develops mold problems, leave it uncovered or partially covered.

If you are gardening on the windowsill or using light fixtures without a frame, such a covering isn't feasible, but you can cover individual pots. Pull a plastic bag over each plant and tuck the bag opening into the top of the pot. Moisture that condenses will run back into the pot, continuing to water the plant. Support the bag inside with stakes so the plastic doesn't touch the leaves. Don't leave covered plants in strong sunlight, or they will be damaged.

note:

Seed is dated when packaged and while most garden centers and seed companies will not sell past-dated seed, they may be willing to donate it to school gardening programs. As long as packets are kept in a cool, dry location, most seeds will germinate well for several years.

DIGGING DEEPER

What About pH?

The pH of the growing medium is an important consideration for growing plants. The pH reflects the acidity or alkalinity of a soil. The pH scale runs from 0 (acid) to 14 (alkaline), with 7.0 being a neutral pH.

The ideal range for growing most vegetable and annual flower plants is between 6.0 and 6.8. If the pH is not within a suitable range, plants cannot take up nutrients. In some cases, certain minerals increase to toxic levels in the soil if the pH is too low.

Commercial soilless mixes have a balanced pH in the appropriate range, so you won't have to be concerned with this when using them.

If you're using garden soil in your potting mix, measure the pH of your mix with a commercial test kit, available through seed companies and garden supply stores. This is an excellent activity for students. You can also use litmus paper to do a simple pH test. If the pH is too low (acid), raise it by adding 3 tablespoons of ground limestone for every 8 gallons of potting mix. If it is too high, use a larger proportion of peat moss in your mix and test again.

Indoor Gardening Supplies

In addition to the materials used to construct the indoor garden you will need basic supplies such as growing media, containers, fertilizer, and plant labels. Plan to purchase "consumable" supplies, such as growing medium and fertilizer, regularly. Other supplies should last for several years. If there are a number of gardening classrooms within your school or school system, consider purchasing in bulk to save money. Many greenhouse and nursery supply catalogs carry pots, soilless mix, and fertilizer in bulk quantities.

You will also need plants. You can fill your indoor garden with plants started from seeds or cuttings, or you can purchase mature plants. Most classrooms begin their gardens by planting seeds because they are relatively inexpensive and their growth helps students to visualize the full life cycle of a plant. You can often get seed donations from local garden centers or seed companies. Chapter 3 provides additional information about planting seeds, and Appendix B provides instructions for starting plants from cuttings.

Choosing a Growing Medium

The growing medium in which you raise your plants is important. It provides a base to anchor the roots so the plants don't fall over. It also serves as a reservoir for the water, air, and nutrients taken up by the roots.

We recommend using a commercial soilless potting mix, made from peat moss, coconut husk fiber, vermiculite, and/or perlite, for a number of reasons:

It is light enough to allow for good water drainage, root aeration, and root growth, yet heavy and spongy enough to provide anchorage and to hold onto adequate water and nutrients.

It's easy to transport and readily available in most garden stores.

It's clean. It doesn't contain weed seeds, insects, or diseases that could flourish in the favorable conditions of an indoor garden.

It is a known quantity. While garden soil-based mixes may vary in pH and in nutrients, soilless mix contains few nutrients and has a stable pH. You control the nutrients your plants receive by applying fertilizer.

It doesn't produce mud. If it gets on clothing, it brushes off easily.

It works. Thousands of school children, teachers, and commercial growers have achieved gardening success with this type of soilless mix.

Packages of soilless mix tend to be small and expensive at discount stores and mailorder suppliers. Local garden supply centers often carry large 4- to 6-cubic-foot bales, one of which should be enough to last three seasons in the average gardening classroom.

Other Growing Mix Options

Once you have become confident of your indoor growing abilities, you can experiment with other types of mixes or additions to the basic mix.

Some people prefer to mix their own soilless or soil-based growing mix since it can be somewhat more economical. Below is a recipe for 8 gallons of a standard soilless growing mix:

Mix thoroughly:
 4 gallons vermiculite
 4 gallons sphagnum peat moss
 4 tablespoons superphosphate (or 1 cup steamed bonemeal)
 4 tablespoons dolomitic limestone

The following list outlines the benefits and drawbacks of adding garden soil, compost, or sand to your growing medium. When adding any of these materials, limit the quantity to one-third the volume of the mix.

Garden soil — Well-drained soil is the only type that should be added to a growing mix.

Advantages: Garden soil often has abundant nutrients, provides additional support, and holds water well.

Disadvantages: It has variable pH, may be too heavy, and can impede drainage. Because it is not sterile, it should ideally be pasteurized in a 180°F oven for forty minutes (this is a smelly process).

Compost — Sift compost through a screen before adding it to a growing mix.

Advantages: Compost has abundant nutrients, provides additional support, and holds water well.

Disadvantages: It has a variable pH and may not be sterile. If not properly composted, pasteurize it as described above.

Sand — Coarse builders' sand is best. Seashore sand may contain harmful salts.

Advantages: It provides additional support and improves drainage.

Disadvantages: Too much sand will cause a mix to dry out rapidly.

Selecting Containers

We recommend 6-inch-diameter plastic pots for use in classroom gardens for several reasons:

The pots are durable. You can wash and reuse them many times and they are easy to clean and sterilize with a bleach solution.

They do not dry out quickly like fiber or clay containers because they are not porous. This can be a particular benefit during school vacations.

They're large enough to accommodate the roots of most of the plants we

Vermiculite, a common ingredient in potting mix, produces dust that can irritate respiratory passages. Moisten your soilless mix before pouring to minimize dust, and pour carefully. Cover your nose and mouth whenever you pour vermiculite.

recommend for indoor gardens, particularly as the plants reach maturity.

They are relatively inexpensive and easily purchased in large quantities from garden stores and mailorder suppliers. Sometimes you can get a good discount by explaining your project to a garden center owner. To get the best price, consider buying in bulk (100 or more) from a nursery or greenhouse supplier. Also ask your students' parents if they have extra pots they'd be willing to donate.

Other Container Options

If you think a different kind of container will be more accessible or appropriate for your indoor garden, read the following comparison of various planting containers. Whichever you use, remember these important points:

Most of the recommended indoor garden plants require at least a 6-inch soil depth to grow to maturity. (Check the Grower's Guide, Appendix A, for information on pot sizes for various crops.)

All containers must have drainage holes in the bottom to avoid water-logging and killing plants. If necessary, punch drainage holes in the bottom of homemade containers before planting.

Market Packs are the standard plastic containers used for seedlings in garden centers.

Advantages: They are readily available (you can easily find people who will donate them), easy to handle, and useful when growing seedlings for sale or to send home.

Disadvantages: They are too small to grow most plants to maturity.

School Milk Cartons are free! Be sure to make drainage holes.

Advantages: They are excellent for growing small plants for children to take home and replant.

Disadvantages: They are too small for growing most plants to maturity.

Shallow Rectangular Growers' Flats are short plastic trays used for planting seeds that will later be transplanted into individual pots.

Advantages: They are good for starting large quantities of closely spaced seeds for later transplanting; you can also use them as beds for growing crops like lettuce, or for starting houseplant cuttings.

Disadvantages: Some don't drain well.

Egg Cartons (cardboard or styrofoam) are free and plentiful. Be sure to make drainage holes.

Advantages: These are fine for starting seedlings that you will immediately transplant to larger containers.

Disadvantages: The cells are very small and dry out quickly.

Plastic Planting Bags are dark plastic bags filled with soilless mix. The bags are perforated on top so that you can sow seeds or insert transplants. They are available from many garden supply stores and catalogs.

Advantages: The plastic keeps plant roots warm and moist, which is good for heat-loving crops.

Disadvantages: They take up quite a bit of space, are hard to reuse, and may not drain well.

Clay Pots are very common in garden stores, and they come in many sizes.

Advantages: The porous material allows soil very good air exchange, reducing the risk of mold problems. They are attractive, and their weight helps stabilize tall or bushy plants.

Disadvantages: They are fairly expensive and heavy, and dry out very rapidly.

Fiber Pots are made by compressing different types of coarse fibers into a bowl shape. They come in a range of shapes and sizes, and are often used for hanging baskets.

Advantages: They are inexpensive and well aerated.

Disadvantages: They have a shorter life span than plastic or clay, and they dry out fairly rapidly.

Plastic Soda Bottle Bottoms are another free resource. Many teachers ask students to bring plastic 2-liter soda bottles to class, where they cut off the tops and punch holes in the bottom to make deep growing containers. They also make good individual terrariums (see Appendix B).

Advantages: They are readily available, free, and provide good soil depth.

Disadvantages: They must be cut apart, and are poorly drained.

Labeling Containers

Once you dive into classroom experiments it's easy to lose track of the names and planting dates of the seeds you started. Use 4- to 6-inch wooden or plastic pot labels (available from garden centers, greenhouse supply catalogs, and seed catalogs) to keep track of this information. You can also use Popsicle sticks from craft stores (your art teacher may have extras) or recycled plastic silverware.

Use waterproof pens to write on your labels. Although they're harder to read, pencils are adequate for writing on most wooden labels.

Fertilizer

To maintain the health of your indoor garden you will need fertilizer. Retail garden centers and discount stores carry a wide range of fertilizers, as do many seed, greenhouse, and nursery supply catalogs. The amount you'll need depends on which fertilizer you choose and the nutrient needs of the plants you grow. See pages 49-51 for detailed information on plant nutrients and fertilizers.

When cleaning pots or other garden equipment with bleach solution, take extra care, especially around children. Bleach is toxic, and can burn skin and damage clothing.

Seeking Financial Support

Once you determine your material and supply needs, you can work on a plan for obtaining them. Many teachers and their students have equipped indoor gardens without making demands on tight budgets by soliciting donations, applying for grants, and launching fundraisers.

Donations

Seeking material and supply donations allows the community to participate in your exciting youth gardening program. Begin with parents — next to their kids, they are the people most strongly invested in your program. They may donate items directly or tap connections in the community to fulfill your needs. Create a classroom newsletter to inform parents of your plans.

Approach organizations directly for donations of new and used gardening materials. Botanical gardens, local garden clubs, university or city greenhouses, local service clubs, and community garden groups are great resources, and may even sponsor or "adopt" your indoor gardening project. Such a partnership can have more than just financial benefits, as students and the organization members share information, exchange correspondence, and develop friendships.

You can also tie the donation search to curriculum standards. Some teachers have students write letters or make presentations to managers of garden supply stores. This is a practical lesson in the power of clear communication. Many classes have found that garden center managers offer both enthusiastic support and sound gardening advice.

When you or your students solicit donations, be sure to explain the objectives of your school gardening project clearly and describe how the donation will be recognized. Also, be sure to follow up all donations (large or small) with timely and enthusiastic thank yous. In many schools where outside organizations have donated, built, or financed GrowLabs, each GrowLab carries a small plaque, visible to all who visit, that lists and thanks the supporters. People who know their gift was appreciated and put to good use are more likely to give again. Great ways of thanking supporters include: heartfelt thank-you letters, drawings from the children, and photographs of abundant indoor gardens surrounded by smiling young faces.

Grants

There are a number of monetary and in-kind grants available to help fund youth gardens. Start your search at the KidsGardening.org Grants page. Grants are available from public funds (local, state, and federal government), private foundations (general, community, corporate, family), and corporations. Some grants are available to groups in specific regions or counties. Here are some tips for finding and applying for grants:

- Make sure grant requirements match your needs. Research programs that a funding organization has supported in the past, and learn its current priorities.

- Give yourself plenty of time to complete the application before the submission deadline.

- Submit a professional application. Follow instructions carefully, answer questions thoroughly, keep text concise and meaningful, emphasize what's unique about your program, and include plans for sustainability.

- Before you submit it, have someone proofread your application. Ask whether your program's goals and purpose are clearly stated and easily understood.

Fundraising

Fundraising provides students with business experience and can satisfy many learning goals. Here are a few ideas:

- Plant and sell vegetable, herb, and flower seedlings.
- Sell potted flowering plants for special occasions.
- Sell certificates for gardening services such as weeding, raking, etc.
- Sell tickets to a salad banquet.

Chapter 3

Planting Your Indoor Garden

O nce you obtain supplies and set up your indoor garden, you and your students will be eager to plant your crops. This chapter will help you plan your garden and prepare your planting equipment. You'll also find step-by-step sowing instructions and tips to help ensure germination.

Planning

Many new gardeners enthusiastically plant an entire packet of radish seeds only to find out, a month later, that they are tending the largest radish plantation in town! Through experience, gardeners learn to plan ahead in order to balance the harvest. Plant just 10 to 20 radish seeds a week and you'll have a constant, manageable harvest over the span of a month. The following are some other important points to consider when planning your classroom garden.

GrowLab: A Complete Guide to Gardening in the Classroom

What Can You Grow Indoors?

The Grower's Guide (Appendix A) includes a list of tried-and-true vegetables, flowers, and herbs that work well for the indoor garden. These recommended crops generally do not take up much space. Most remain under 2 feet high and will produce abundantly when grown in 6-inch diameter pots. If you have a windowsill garden, choose plants from the list that have low light requirements.

You can also grow common houseplants, blooming bulbs, and tropical fruits. An indoor garden is an excellent environment for starting all types of seedlings, cuttings, and bulbs. For a selection of indoor garden ideas, complete with planting instructions, refer to Special Projects for Indoor Gardens (Appendix B).

Remember, not all garden crops are good candidates for indoor growing. Corn is too tall. Spinach is too sensitive to heat. Acorn squash takes up too much space.

What Do You Want to Grow?

This will depend on the goals you set for your classroom garden. We recommend that first-time indoor gardeners start small and try some relatively foolproof crops, such as radishes, lettuce, beans, marigolds, and dwarf tomatoes. (Read Chapter 1 before choosing your plants, since this may affect your choices.)

The planning stage of gardening is an opportunity to involve the whole class in the decision-making process and to learn about the childrens' food preferences and ethnic backgrounds. It makes sense to include some "sure-fire" crops and some class favorites. Some teachers include one or two experimental, unfamiliar items like peanuts or cotton for fun.

How Much and When Should You Plant?

The Growers' Guide (Appendix A) indicates the number of seeds of each recommended crop to plant in each pot, and the approximate number of weeks until maturity. Work backwards from your harvest plans to determine your seed-sowing date, and consider these questions:

How much of each crop will you need in the end? Consult the Growers' Guide to determine the number of pots of each crop to plant. For instance, if you're planning a salad party for a class of thirty, assume that one small plant will feed each student. The Growers' Guide indicates that you can plant four lettuce plants per 6-inch pot, so you'll need to plant eight pots of lettuce. You can plan the same way for the rest of the salad vegetables.

When do you want to have your harvest or finish your experiments? Once you've answered this question and used the Growers' Guide, you can determine when to plant each crop so it will be ready as needed. If you are planning for a coordinated harvest, remember that crops take different amounts of time to mature, so plan accordingly (see Table 1 on page 20 for a sample planning guide).

Many teachers find it helpful to harvest crops and conclude experiments just before a school vacation so they don't have to leave the classroom garden unattended.

Curriculum Planning

What you decide to grow in your indoor garden will depend on your students' interests, your time and space limitations, and your curriculum goals. You might use the GrowLab as a context for plant growth experiments, or for thematic units on herbs, plant adaptations, rainforests, and so on. KidsGardening's 307-page curriculum guide, **GrowLab: Activities for Growing Minds,** will help you plan and facilitate age-appropriate investigations that help students discover important life science concepts covering basic needs, reproduction, diversity, adaptations, and interdependence.

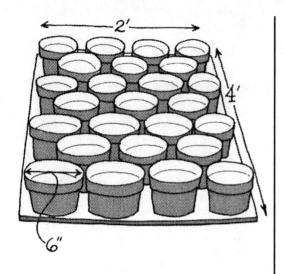

How can you make the best use of your growing space? Approximately twenty-five 6-inch pots can fit in a standard 2-by-4-foot Grow Lab at one time (although you may choose fewer, larger plants).

Think about planting dates and days to maturity to maximize use of your space. If you plant short-season crops, like radishes and lettuce, you may have time to plant and harvest a second crop before school ends.

Sample Planning Calendar

Some teachers find it helpful to draw up a full-year planning calendar for the indoor garden. One fourth-grade teacher drew up the following calendar to outline major garden activities and planting dates.

September — Assemble GrowLab; write letters to seed companies; start houseplant cuttings for Thanksgiving gifts.

October — Conduct germination experiments; sow long-season crops (tomatoes, peppers, carrots) for Valentine's Day salad party; make sprouts for tasting; discuss World Food Day.

November — Start growth charts and records; begin fertilizer experiments; bring home houseplant gifts.

December — Sow more seeds for salad party (lettuce, cucumbers, and beans); prepare garden for vacation; final reports on fertilizer experiment due.

January — Start marigold seeds for Mother's Day gifts; plant "mystery" seed; start nutrition unit; study pollination and hand pollinate cucumbers.

February — Design and produce menus for Valentine's Day harvest salad party.

March — Start seedlings for outdoor garden and spring plant sale; field trip to herb farm.

April — Transplant seedlings to larger containers; begin unit on water cycles.

May — Spring plant sale; bring home Mother's Day flowers; transplant seedlings outdoors.

June — Use proceeds from plant sale for field trip to botanical gardens. Clean and disassemble GrowLab.

Planting

Once you've decided what to plant, how much of each crop to plant, and when to plant each one, you and your students will be ready to dive in. It's handy to set aside an area of the classroom for potting and planting, ideally close to a water source. In some classrooms, kids cover their desks with newspaper or large plastic bags, and prepare pots and plant seeds there.

When planting time comes, you'll either plant directly into permanent containers, or you'll sow seeds into containers from which you will later transplant seedlings.

Sowing into Permanent Pots

You and your students will start some seeds in their permanent pots, either because they are crops that do not transplant well (see list below) or because you choose not to take the extra time to transplant with the class.

There are a number of plants whose tender root systems are shocked or damaged from transplanting. Although the classroom garden environment is more forgiving than the outdoors, and there is less chance of seedlings being set back by transplanting, the following crops should always be sown directly into their permanent containers:

Beans	Squash
Peas	Carrots
Cucumbers	Beets
Melons	Radishes

Sowing for Later Transplanting

You may want to sow seeds into temporary pots and transplant them later for a number of reasons:

Transplanting is an important and exciting gardening practice.

Tiny seeds are hard to handle and place where you want them.

Scattering small seeds (like those of petunia and impatiens) and transplanting them later makes sense.

Transplanting can be a space-saving activity. For instance, if your indoor garden is full and you want to start some seeds to take the place of maturing plants, sow them thickly in a shallow container and give them a head start. When you transplant them, you can choose to transplant only the healthiest ones so weaker plants won't take up space under the lights.

Some plants actually benefit from transplanting. These include tomatoes, lettuce, peppers, and onions. Since a tomato plant develops small roots along its stem where the stem touches soil, transplanting it so that its stem is deep in the soil increases the number of roots it will develop. This, in turn, increases nutrient uptake and anchorage.

How to Plant Your Indoor Garden

1. Gather your planting materials, including:
   - water source
   - nonporous container (plastic bucket or plastic bag within a wastebasket for mixing the soilless mix)
   - planting containers
   - clean soilless or other potting mix*
   - seed packets
   - potting labels (e.g., wooden popsicle sticks or plastic markers)

*It's best not to reuse potting mix once you've grown plants in it. In the warm, moist environment of the indoor garden, used potting mix may pass on disease or pest problems. You **can** reuse potting mix in compost piles or to repot houseplants or other well-established plants, which are less susceptible to pests and disease.

Certain seeds, such as beans and squash, are susceptible to fungus problems. To prevent fungus growth, suppliers often treat these seeds with a fungicide and dye them (usually pink) for identification. The fungicide is toxic, but it may make the seeds look appealing to kids. Seed packets and seed catalogs should indicate if seeds are treated, so choose untreated seeds when possible. Other-wise, store seeds carefully, warn children of the danger, and wash hands thoroughly after handlingtreated seeds.

– waterproof maker or pencil
– spray bottle, watering can with sprinkling head, squeeze bottle, or plant mister
– slow-release fertilizer (optional)

2. **Measure the amount of soilless mix that you'll need.** Use one of your 6-inch pots as a measure to put the mix into your mixing container. Throw in a little extra so you don't run short.

3. **If you are using slow-release fertilizer, add it to the mix and distribute it evenly.**

4. **Pour in about a third as much warm water as you have soilless mix.** The mixture is very absorbent and is much easier to work with when pre-moistened. Continue adding water and mixing with your hands until the mixture is evenly moist throughout. Squeeze some in your fist. If water drips out, the mix is too wet. When properly moistened, the mix will form a ball in your hand and crumble when touched. If it's too wet, either add more mix, or leave the containers uncovered to let water evaporate.

If you have the time, moisten the mix and leave it overnight in a closed container to allow it to absorb water more completely. If you can't use the moistened mix the next day, keep it covered so it doesn't dry out. Don't use mix that has been moistened for more than a week, since it may begin to develop harmful fungus.

5. **If you are using pots with very large drainage holes,** line just the bottom of each container with a single thickness of newsprint or paper towel (see illustration). This will prevent the potting mix from falling out through the drainage holes. Don't use shiny newspaper or magazines, as some have coatings that are toxic. Don't leave the paper sticking up above the soil in the pot, as it will wick moisture away from the soil and plant roots.

6. **Fill the container with moistened mix.** Press the mix down lightly with your hand or another container and leave at least 1 inch of headroom at the top. This space will make watering easier, and will allow you to add more mix later on to help cover exposed roots and stabilize stems.

7. **Sow seeds. If seeds are extremely fine,** sprinkle them on the soil surface and pat them into the soil (see figure A, page 41). To ensure a better distribution, first mix fine seeds with sand or a little potting mix.

If seeds are larger, sow them in shallow furrows or individual small holes. The general rule is to plant seeds at a depth of three times the width of the seed.

If you are sowing seeds directly into their permanent containers, refer to the Growers' Guide and space the correct number of seeds evenly around the pot (see figure B). Because it is unreasonable to expect 100 percent germination from a batch of seed, put two seeds in each planting hole.

If you are planting closely for later transplanting, space the seeds 1/4 inch apart in rows 1 or 2 inches apart (see figure C). You will transplant seedlings while they're still small, before the roots become intertwined.

8. **Cover the seeds with soil unless they are tiny.** Pat them gently into the soil surface to maximize conduction of water between soil and seed.

9. **Moisten the soil again carefully with a plant mister, squeeze bottle, or gentle sprinkler head** (to avoid washing the seeds away).

10. **Make a wooden, plastic, or masking tape label.** Use a waterproof marker or pencil to list the date, the plant variety, and if appropriate, the name or initials of the student gardener.

11. **Cover the container with clear plastic or wax paper** (see figure D). This will create a greenhouse effect and maintain moist conditions during germination. Don't let the covering rest on the soil or you'll pull out the tender seedlings when you remove the cover. Avoid this by supporting the cover with pot labels or toothpicks, or using a rubber band to hold it taut across the top of the pot.

12. **Place the containers in the indoor garden or another warm spot in the room.** If your room is on the cold side or your planting area is near cold windows, you can put the containers near, but not on, a heat source (e.g., radiator, ducts). Watch closely to make sure pots don't get too hot and dry. Be ready to place them under lights or by a sunny window as soon as the seeds germinate.

13. **Store leftover seeds in a sealed container** (film canister, glass jar, envelope) and keep them in a cool, dry place until you need them. You can add some cornmeal or rice to a glass jar, then place seed packets in the jar. The grain will absorb excess moisture. If stored properly, most seeds will keep for several years. Your class can perform germination tests to check the viability of seeds before planting (see Digging Deeper, page 43).

Germination Secrets

Two important conditions required for successful seed germination (sprouting) are moisture and warmth.

Moisture

Keep seeds in your indoor garden consistently moist until they germinate. Covering containers with clear plastic or wax paper will maintain moisture and allow the children to see the germination process. Remember that the cover shouldn't touch the soil. If the soil mix seems to be drying out, water with a plant mister or very gentle watering head to avoid washing seeds away.

Check containers daily. Remove the covering as soon as seedlings sprout and set the containers under lights. Begin to water seedlings as described on page 48.

Warmth

A GrowLab, warm windowsill, or spot near a heating source will provide adequate warmth for the germination of most indoor garden plants. You won't need to monitor germination temperatures for different plants, although different seeds germinate within different temperature ranges (see Table 3 for examples).

figure A

figure B

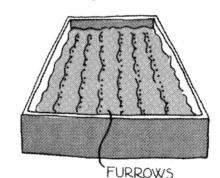

FURROWS
1-2" APART

figure C

figure D

Never place containers directly on top of fluorescent lights, radiators, or other heating or electrical devices.

If the temperature in your classroom falls below 50°F for extended periods of time over weekends or vacations, consider using a heating cable or a propagating mat in the base of your garden. These will warm the soil to temperatures sufficient for germination.

Table 3 lists the range of germination temperatures for a selection of indoor garden vegetables. This table will help your students predict when their seeds will germinate. You can use this information to have students place "bets" and turn their predictions into a game.

Germination Temperatures for Selected Vegetables
(in Degrees Fahrenheit)   Table 3

Crop	Minimum	Ideal Range	Maximum
Beans	60	70-85	95
Beets	40	65-75	95
Carrots	40	60-70	95
Cucumbers	60	70-80	105
Lettuce	35	45-65	85
Peppers	60	70-75	95
Tomatoes	50	70-75	95

Table 4 illustrates the effect of soil temperature on the rate of seed germination, using carrots as an example. With a soil thermometer (purchased at a garden supply store or from a mailorder supplier), conduct classroom experiments to test the effect of temperature on the germination of other crops, too.

Effect of Soil Temperature on Rate of Germination (Carrots)   Table 4

Temperature – Degrees Fahrenheit	Days to Germination
95	8.6
77	6.2
68	6.9
50	17.3
41	50.6

Light

Most of your seeds will sprout with or without light. Children should carefully observe containers, however, since they'll need to place the seedlings under lights as soon as they emerge from the soil.

Germination Failure

There are a number of reasons why seeds fail to germinate. If you have a problem with germination refer to this list:

- – Soil temperature too low or too high
- – Soil dried out
- – Seeds planted too deeply
- – Seeds washed away during watering
- – Seeds too old and/or improperly stored
- – Poor soil-to-seed contact
- – Damping off disease

Don't become discouraged if you have poor germination. Try again right away with clean containers and fresh mix. You will probably be successful on your second try. Remember also that some seeds germinate very quickly and others take longer, so check the Growers' Guide (Appendix A) for approximate germination times.

Germination Tests

To see if old seeds are worth replanting, conduct germination tests with your class. For each type of seed being tested, lay out ten seeds on a moist paper towel. Cover them with a second sheet of moist paper towel, making a "sandwich." Fold up the towel sandwich like an accordion, moisten again, place it in a plastic bag, and put the bag in a warm place out of direct sunlight.

After a week or ten days, unroll each towel and have children count the number of seeds, out of ten, that have germinated. Then calculate a percentage of germination. If fewer than 50 percent of seeds sprout, use fresh seed or sow seed thickly to compensate for the low germination rate.

Chapter 4

Maintaining a Healthy Indoor Garden

Whether you're gardening on a windowsill or in a GrowLab, the environment must meet four specific plant needs if your plants are to thrive. This chapter describes these basic needs — light, heat, water, and nutrients — and explains how to meet them in your indoor garden. Although different plants have specific needs for ideal growth, you can achieve healthy plants by offering an average of what most plants need for reasonable growth. You'll also find instructions for thinning, transplanting, and pollinating, and advice for caring for your plants over long breaks and holidays.

Remember, there are a number of lessons to be learned from failures as well as successes in the garden. Even with the most careful garden management, plants sometimes fail to thrive. Accidents happen. Pests or diseases cause crop failure. Seeds may fail to germinate. But a failure of one sort or another can become the focus for a new lesson or experiment. For example, if your beans develop a mold and the plants die, seize the opportunity to investigate the life of molds. Use magnifying glasses and microscopes to examine them. Find out what conditions they need to thrive. Try growing molds on different substances. Learn about helpful molds. Then, using what you've learned about the optimum growth conditions for mold, replant and provide conditions that will discourage mold and result in healthy plants.

Light

Plants can't grow without light, so providing proper lighting conditions is critical to the success of your indoor garden. Using the right type and number of tubes, as described on page 28, is just the beginning. You also need to consider light intensity and duration, and then follow the height and time recommendations in this section to provide adequate light for a thriving garden.

Intensity

Light intensity, or the amount of light a plant receives, affects all aspects of growth and development. Intensity varies based on the type of light used and the distance between the light and the plants. The closer the light is to a plant, the higher the intensity. Light intensity is measured in terms of footcandles. A footcandle is the amount of light produced in a totally dark space by one candle shining on a white surface that is 1 square foot in size, 1 foot from the candle.

Most of the flowers, vegetables, and herbs you'll grow indoors do quite well with the 1,000 to 1,500 footcandles of light provided by six fluorescent tubes, and some will do well with quite a bit less. By contrast, 50 footcandles is average office light, and the light at noon outdoors on a sunny day might be as bright as 10,000 footcandles.

The amount of light your indoor garden receives will depend on many factors, including the time of year, orientation of the window, and proximity of lights to a reflective surface. Placing your light garden near a white wall or backing it with aluminum foil increases, through reflection, the amount of light available to your plants. Your class can investigate various ways to increase light intensity by using a light meter to check the results of your efforts.

Adjusting Light Height

Always keep tubes 3 to 6 inches from the tops of the plants to foster good plant growth. The amount of light reaching your plants drops drastically as you raise the lights, so resist the temptations to keep lights high for good viewing. If your lights are on adjustable chains, you can raise them easily while children are watering, inspecting plants, or conducting investigations. If your plants are very tall and spindly looking, your lights are probably too high.

Since you will have plants of varying heights but will still want to maintain light at the proper distance, you should arrange plants according to height with some lights higher than others. Another way to adjust height is to place short plants on top of upturned pots.

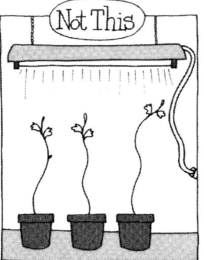

Measuring Light Intensity

One class of eighth-grade students used the light meter in a camera to measure the intensity (footcandles) of light available to plants in various parts of the room and at various distances from the light tubes. This is the procedure they used:

Set the film speed at ASA 200 and the shutter speed at $1/125$ second. Aim the camera at a white sheet of paper where your plants will be located. Get close enough so the meter records only light reflected from the paper. Be careful not to create shadows.

Focus on the paper and adjust the f-stop until a correct exposure shows in the light meter of the camera. F-stops will equal approximate footcandles as follows:

F-Stop	Footcandles
2.8	32
4.0	64
5.6	125
8.0	250
11.0	500
16.0	1,000
22.0	2,000

Do not angle the lights so that one end is higher than the other. This is unsafe since water could condense and run down to the light terminal, creating the danger of electric shock.

How Plants Can Live in an Enclosed System

After helping to build a class terrarium, one thoughtful fifth-grade student asked, "If we need oxygen (which plants give off) and plants need carbon dioxide (which we give off), how can plants survive in an enclosed terrarium?" If you study the cycles described below in Understanding Photosynthesis, you'll notice that plants both photosynthesize **and** respire. During respiration they produce the carbon dioxide that they need for photosynthesis. The decay of plant matter also produces carbon dioxide. Thus, technically, we cannot live without plants, but they can live perfectly well without us!

Understanding Photosynthesis

Life on earth is completely dependent on the food and oxygen produced by plants and a few other organisms during the process of photosynthesis.

Photosynthesis is the process by which plants containing green chlorophyll employ the energy of the light to combine carbon dioxide (CO_2) from the air with hydrogen (H) from water (H_2O) to produce sugars.

The relatively simple sugars produced through photosynthesis are later built into more complex plant foods such as starches, fats, and proteins.

Some of the food produced by a plant during photosynthesis is temporarily stored in the leaves. The remainder is transported through the stem to other parts of the plant where it is stored until needed. This food energy might be stored in a number of forms — as a starch (in potatoes) or as a fat (in peanuts), for example.

The plant eventually uses the stored food to produce more foliage, roots, stems, flowers, and ultimately, to produce offspring, thus beginning the cycle again.

Many of your teaching materials have further explanations of photosynthesis and respiration. Use those references to make these concepts part of your GrowLab lessons.

Light intensity is much greater at the center of your tubes than at the several inches on either end and therefore is greater in the middle of the GrowLab than near the edges. Rotate your plants every couple of weeks to ensure that all plants have a chance to receive adequate lighting.

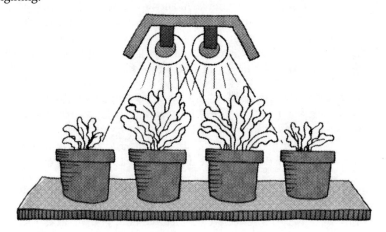

Controlling Light Duration

Light duration is as important as light intensity. **Outdoor garden plants need an average of six to eight hours of sunlight, but because light intensity is lower indoors, indoor garden plants need fourteen to sixteen hours of light per day.** Use a timer to turn the lights on and off automatically, providing consistent light for your indoor garden. Do not leave lights on twenty-four hours a day. More light will not cause plants to produce more abundantly. Plants actually require a period of darkness each day in order for respiration to occur. Respiration is the process whereby plants convert the products of photosynthesis into usable energy.

Windowsill Light

The amount of light your plants receive on a windowsill depends on the direction the window faces, whether the sun is blocked by trees or a building, the number of cloudy days, and how much overhang your roof has. Another consideration with windowsill plants is the duration of light. During most of the school year, even the best south-facing window will receive fewer than the fourteen to sixteen hours we recommend.

Given the light limitations of most windowsill gardens, your best plant options are houseplants, herbs, and leaf and root vegetables. These do not need the high levels of light required by fruiting and flowering plants. Here are some recommendations:

beets	radishes	onion tops
carrots	herbs	mustard
garlic	flowering bulbs	fruit tree seedlings
lettuce	foliage houseplants	

On a sill, light comes from only one direction, so you'll need to rotate your plants every couple of days as they begin to lean toward the light. Your class can investigate this movement toward light, called phototropism. Set up experiments indoors and identify the process outdoors in the environment.

Heat

In the previous chapter, you learned that seeds germinate best within a certain range of temperatures, and the same goes for overall plant growth. Generally, the optimal air temperature for growing the mature plants is slightly less than that for germinating seeds.

Temperatures between 60° and 80°F are adequate for germinating and growing most indoor garden plants. Ideally, night temperatures for most plants should be 10 to 15 degrees cooler than the day temperatures. Both of these day and night ranges are typical of most classrooms. If you use a plastic or foil covering to maintain humidity in your indoor garden, it also will help to keep the air surrounding your plants slightly warmer than room temperature.

If your school sets the thermostat to a very low setting over a winter vacation, use a heating cable or seedling heating mat to maintain the temperatures in your classroom garden. Use heating cables or mats only for germination or to maintain a reasonable temperature in the garden. Too much heat can cause plants to dry out quickly. When using a heating cable, be sure to keep the base material moist and when using a heating mat, make sure to follow the manufacturer's instructions. (See Appendix D for information on how to set up a heating cable.)

Water

Plants cannot survive without water. It carries nutrients through the soil, into the roots, and up through the plant to places where the plant can use the nutrients. Water is important for photosynthesis and transpiration. It also helps keep the plants erect, enabling them to take advantage of light for photosynthesis.

Too little water causes wilting, decreases nutrient transport and photosynthesis, and eventually leads to death of the plant.

Too much water prevents air exchange around the roots, which essentially suffocates them and causes them to rot. Roots that have to search a little for water become stronger than those that are overwatered. **Overwatering can cause as many problems as underwatering!**

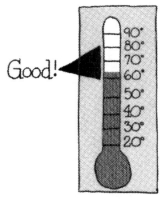

Good!

DIGGING DEEPER

Cool and Warm Weather Crops

In outdoor gardens, we distinguish between cool and warm weather crops. As the terms indicate, cool-season crops are those which produce best growth, or will mature only during cool temperatures (40° to 65°F). Warm-season crops require warmer temperatures (above 65°F) for best growth. Since classroom temperatures tend to be warm, there are certain cool weather crops, like spinach and peas, that can be quite difficult to grow indoors. Others, like lettuce, will grow nicely indoors but may become bitter when temperatures are too warm.

You can grow all of the crops listed in the Grower's Guide (Appendix A) successfully in an indoor environment. If you have extreme temperature conditions in your classroom, choose crops accordingly. Below is a list of some common cool and warm weather crops you can grow indoors:

Cool	Warm
peas	tomatoes
radishes	peppers
lettuce	eggplant
carrots	beans
snapdragons	peanuts
	cucumbers
	marigolds
	basil
	zinnias

If you're using a heating cable as described in Appendix D, you should keep the base material constantly moist. This will help conduct the heat to the root zone of the plants.

Watering Your Garden

It's best to water only when the plants need it rather than on a set schedule. Large plants with lots of leaves use water faster than small plants. Porous planting containers, like clay pots, will lose water much more quickly than solid (plastic) containers. Soil dries out more quickly when classroom temperatures are high. (Pay close attention to water needs when using a heating cable.)

To tell when your plants need water, stick your finger about an inch into the soil in a pot. If soil adheres to it and/or feels moist, you do not need to water yet. Be sure to check a number of pots. Some classes purchase water meters at garden stores and compare the instrument readings with the students' own subjective readings.

When you water, give each plant enough to wet the soil thoroughly. Add water until it seeps out from the bottom of the pot.

When watering young seedlings, use a gentle sprinkling head or a hand-held sprayer to avoid washing them away.

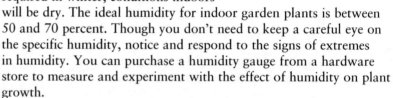

Controlling Humidity

The humidity in your classroom will fluctuate a great deal. If you live in an arid climate or where heating is required in winter, conditions indoors will be dry. The ideal humidity for indoor garden plants is between 50 and 70 percent. Though you don't need to keep a careful eye on the specific humidity, notice and respond to the signs of extremes in humidity. You can purchase a humidity gauge from a hardware store to measure and experiment with the effect of humidity on plant growth.

Table 5 lists plant symptoms resulting from an excess or deficiency of humidity and ways to address these problems.

Water and electricity don't mix. Raise lights when watering so that watering is done beneath, not above the light fixtures. Some teachers prefer to remove pots from the garden during watering. If fixtures do get wet, unplug or turn off the lights immediately. Allow lights to dry thoroughly before you turn them on again.

Regulating Humidity   Table

Humidity Too High	Humidity Too Low
Symptoms:	**Symptoms:**
White fungus or green algae growth on soil or base material	Leaves curl downward, tips brown
How to lower humidity:	**How to raise humidity:**
– Partially remove covering (plastic or foil) from your garden to increase air circulation.	– Keep the garden covered with plastic or foil.
– Let the base material in the garden dry out.	– Keep the base material evenly moist.
– Cut back on frequency of watering.	– Cluster pots together
– Thin plants (don't crowd them).	
– Create breezes (open window or run a fan)	If you do not have a GrowLab, set your pots of plants in a tray filled with 1 inch of pebbles, perlite, or sand, and add water. As water evaporates, it will raise humidity around the plants.

Nutrients

For healthy growth, all plants require certain nutrients that normally come from the soil. The three primary nutrients are nitrogen (N), phosphorus (P), and potassium (K). Other nutrients are also important, but plants require them in much smaller amounts. Soilless mixes may contain some nutrients to get plants off to a good start, but you will have to fertilize your plants regularly to maintain healthy plant growth.

We recommend a complete water-soluble liquid fertilizer for use with indoor gardens for several reasons:

- It is widely available in garden stores and catalogs.
- It is relatively inexpensive.
- It is rapidly available to plants and the concentration can be easily controlled.

Three numbers on a fertilizer label (5-10-5, for example) represent the percentages of nitrogen (5 percent), phosphorus (10 percent), and potassium (5 percent) in an available form in that particular fertilizer. These three nutrients are always listed in the same order: nitrogen, phosphorus, potassium. Use a fertilizer with equal amounts of nitrogen, phosphorus, and potassium in your indoor garden, such as 10-10-10, or with a higher percentage of phosphorus, such as 15-30-15.

Table 6 provides a list of functions of these three plant nutrients, and symptoms of deficiencies and excesses of each. (This table simplifies what are actually very complex nutrient functions.)

Fertilizing Your Garden

Follow the directions on the fertilizer label to determine proper dilution and frequency of fertilizing. Overfertilizing can be as harmful as underfertilizing.

Dilution rates vary by product. Manufacturers of most liquid and water-soluble fertilizers recommend fertilizing every two weeks with a full strength dose. Some teachers prefer fertilizing with one-fourth the suggested strength every time they water. This requires less attention than remembering when to fertilize. It's often convenient to mix up a large batch of fertilizer in plastic gallon milk jugs and pour that into the watering can as needed. Make sure fertilizer is kept in a secure location, since it is toxic if ingested.

Start fertilizing only after the first true leaf appears on the plant. The initial two "leaves" are actually cotyledons — the part of the seed that contains nutrients to support the plant's early development.

note:

Misting leaves can help clean dust from plant pores. If you mist, do so lightly and early in the day since wet foliage at night can create pest and disease problems. Do not mist plants with hairy leaves and stems such as tomatoes and African violets.

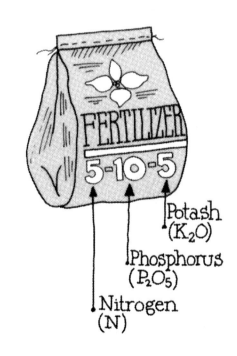

Nutrient Functions, and Symptoms of Deficiencies and Excesses — Table 6

Nutrient	Function	Deficiency Symptoms	Excess Symptoms
Nitrogen (N)	necessary for foliage, growth	yellowing of leaves, beginning with the youngest	long, weak stems and lush, thin foliage, failure to flower
Phosphorus (P)	necessary for root growth, flowering, and fruiting	development of deep green or purplish hue on lower leaves	(not apparent)
Potassium (K)	contributes to overall vigor and resistance	slow growth, stunting, and browning of leaves	(not apparent)

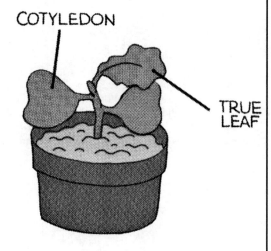

COTYLEDON

TRUE LEAF

Fertilizer is made of concentrated mineral salts and chemicals that can be dangerous if taken internally. Colorful, water-soluble fertilizers might tempt young gardeners. Slow-release fertilizer beads are easily ingested, and could be a hazard. Store these fertilizers out of the reach of children, and discuss these safety issues early on with the class. If a child ingests fertilizer, call a poison center immediately. Do not induce vomiting unless advised to do so by a doctor or poison center.

Fertilizer Options

Below is a description and comparison of some fertilizer options.

Organic Liquid Fertilizers — Fish emulsion, seaweed, and combinations of these are commonly used fertilizers. The concentration of nutrients is lower than in synthetic fertilizers, but the instructions for application compensate for this difference.

Advantages: Nutrients are rapidly available to plants but less concentrated so there is less chance of overfertilizing. Many contain other important trace nutrients and natural plant growth enhancers.

Disadvantages: Many have a disagreeable smell, so look for those labeled "deodorized." They are more expensive in the long run than other water-soluble liquids.

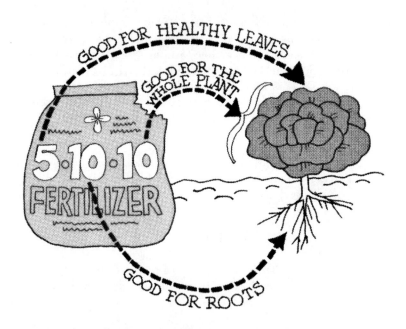

Slow-Release Fertilizers — These are generally beads of fertilizer that slowly release nutrients as the beads decay. You can stir slow-release fertilizer into your potting mix when you initially prepare the soil, or apply it on the surface after planting. Most brands continue to release nutrients for three to four months or more, depending on temperature and moisture. The more often you water the plants, the more quickly fertilizer is released. Warm water also hastens fertilizer release.

Advantages: They require no attention or additional fertilizing for three or four months after the initial mixing.

Disadvantages: Young children may be tempted to put beads into their mouths (the beads are toxic). The availability of nutrients is less controlled and they will be depleted before long-term crops are ready to harvest (you can then add additional fertilizer beads, or water with a liquid fertilizer). There is a danger of overfertilizing plants and causing a buildup of harmful nutrient salts if you use too much water, or water that's too warm.

Compost or Soil in Potting Mix — While soilless mixes have many advantages, potting mixes that contain some compost or soil

are common.

Advantages: Compost and soil contain many trace elements and beneficial organisms, are less expensive than commercial fertilizers, and more closely approximate outside soil conditions.

Disadvantages: They increase the possibility of pest and disease problems and can make the mix too heavy. You will have less precise control over nutrient amounts. You'll need to pasteurize compost and soil by heating small batches in an oven at 180°F for thirty to forty minutes (this decreases nutrient availability and smells bad).

Thinning

It's common practice to plant more seeds than needed, and to plant them closer than recommended, because you can't expect all the seeds to germinate. If too many do spout, the resulting seedlings will be too close together. They'll compete for water and nutrients, and suffer from decreased air circulation and increased risk of disease and pest problems. If left this way, few seedlings, if any, will be healthy. The solution is to thin them.

To thin, gardeners remove seedlings from clumps that are growing too close together. This allows the remaining seedlings more room and better conditions for growth. Thinning is an often-overlooked and disliked task. After all, how can we bear to pull out any of our precious seedlings?

We must bear it, because failure to thin plants is a common reason for poor plant growth in both indoor and outdoor gardens. The sooner you thin, the better. The longer you wait, the more time the plants will have had to compete, the harder it will be to avoid disturbing the other plants, and the more attached you and the children will have gotten to the plants.

How to Thin:

1. **Identify the healthiest looking plants and thin out the rest.** Do this as soon as it's obvious you have too many plants crowded together (once the first true leaves have formed). Check the Growers' Guide (Appendix A) to see how many plants should remain in each container, and thin to that number. Teachers should oversee the thinning process carefully, since it's easy to become overzealous or careless when thinning.

2. **The most benign way to thin crops is to transplant them into other containers** (remember that not all crops transplant well). If you don't have room in the class to keep them, you can give them as gifts to other classrooms or send them home with the children.

   Another method of thinning is to cut off the unwanted plants with your fingernail just above the soil line. The bottom of the plant will eventually die. This is preferable to pulling out plants to be culled, since the pulling may disturb the roots of the remaining plants. Older students can use scissors for this task as well.

3. **Add additional soilless mix to the pot if you have thinned root crops like radishes, turnips, or carrots.** Add enough to cover the roots (they tend to heave up out of the soil in this light mix).

A Creative Lesson on Thinning

One second-grade teacher used role playing to teach children about the difficult task of thinning. She had a group of eight children stand very close together in front of the room and asked them to imagine that they were lettuce plants growing very tightly in a pot. She asked some on the outside to bend and cast a shadow over the others and told the eight "plants" that they would have one glass of water and one sandwich to share among themselves.

The "lettuce plants" were then asked how it felt to be so tightly packed and to share that small amount of food and water. How long did they think they could survive like that? The children began to relate this to the discussion of plants. One of the other students then selected five of the "plants" to thin out and transplant to the other pots. Then all the "plants" stretched out and described what it felt like to have room to grow!

This will improve the root quality at harvest, since exposed roots become dry and scaly.

4. **Water again.** You may have disturbed plant roots during thinning, and watering will settle soil around them.

5. **Your class can enjoy eating the resulting thinnings of crops with edible leaves,** such as lettuce, mustard, beets, parsley, onions, and herbs. No sense in letting your hard work go to waste!

Transplanting

Transplanting is the process of moving young plants from containers in which you first sowed seed or rooted cuttings into new, usually larger, containers or an outdoor garden. (It's also common to transplant houseplants into fresh soil annually, though some do not require transplanting so often.) Refer to Table 2 (page 22) to find out which crops can withstand transplanting. Carefully transferring plants into new, more comfortable homes can be a thrilling experience for youngsters. Read through the following steps to improve transplanting success.

How to Transplant

1. **Transplant only after seedlings show their first true leaves.** The first leaves to appear after germination are the seed leaves or cotyledons. They look different than the normal plant leaves; their job is to provide food to the plant until the true leaves are available to make food through photosynthesis. A week or so after the cotyledons have appeared, true leaves that are more characteristic of the plant will begin to emerge. Once these true leaves appear, it's time to transplant your seedlings. You can wait a couple of weeks, but don't wait much longer because roots will develop and intertwine, making it difficult to lift seedlings without some damage to the roots.

2. **Prepare containers for transplants.** Clean previously used containers with a bleach solution of 1/2 cup bleach to 1 gallon of water and rinse them with clean water to remove any bleach residue. Fill containers with moistened soilless mix, leaving an inch of headroom.

3. **Use your finger or a pencil to make planting holes in the soil.** Holes should be deep enough to accommodate the fully extended roots of the seedlings, and wide enough to allow you to lower these seedlings into the holes.

4. **Grasp a seedling by one of the seed leaves.** (If a seed leaf is torn off, the plant won't be harmed.) Pulling on the leaf gently, coax the seedling out of the soil with a pencil, potting label, toothpick, or similar tool. Don't grasp the seedling by the stem; although stem may seem stronger than the seed leaf, it is much more important to the plant. If the stem is damaged, circulation to the upper part of the plant is shut off and the plant dies.

5. **Lower the seedling into a planting hole.** Use the pencil or potting label to tease the roots down into the hole and to spread them out as much as possible.

6. **Gently press the potting mix around and into the hole with your**

fingers or potting tool.

7. **Once you've filled the pot with transplants, water thoroughly.** This gives the plant plenty of moisture to start with and also helps settle the potting mix around the roots.

8. **Put a label in the pot to identify variety and dates of planting and transplanting.**

Pollinating

Pollination is the process by which the pollen from the tip of the stamen (called the anther) of a male flower is transferred to the tip of the pistil (called the stigma) of a female flower so that fertilization, and then fruit and seed production, can occur, thus completing the full life cycle of a plant. (See the Flower Power worksheet in Appendix C.)

In a garden, pollination is only necessary for producing a harvest of edible fruit or seeds, as with cucumbers or tomatoes. If we eat the root or leaves of a plant (e.g., carrots and lettuce) there is no need for pollination in order to achieve harvest. In nature, pollination is most often completed by the action of wind and insects. In your indoor garden, these plants will probably need your help.

Most flowers are bisexual — that is, they have stamens and pistils in the same blossom (these are called "perfect" flowers). Pollination occurs easily in perfect flowers since their parts are arranged to enable pollen to transfer easily. The slightest touch or air movement around most perfect flowers will lead to pollination. Indoor garden crops that have perfect flowers such as tomatoes, peppers, eggplant, peas, and beans, require only slight movement to pollinate themselves. Normal care such as watering and moving pots, along with air movement in the classroom, will usually provide enough movement to ensure pollination.

Other species, such as cucumbers and squash, have separate male and female blossoms, called "imperfect" flowers. These plants depend on pollinators, including bees, beetles, and moths, to move pollen from anther to stigma. You can recognize the female blossoms by the miniature fruit (ovary) developing behind them, even before pollination occurs. Since squash is not recommended for indoor production, cucumbers are the only crop that you will need to pollinate by hand to simulate the role of insects.

Pollinating Cucumbers Indoors

Since there are (hopefully!) no bees in your classroom to carry the pollen from the male to the female flowers of your cucumbers, you and the children must fill that role. First, you'll need to distinguish the male flower from the female flower. As the plants flower, you will notice that some of the blossoms have a miniature fruit (ovary) at the base. These are the female flowers.

Although this miniature fruit looks like the beginning of a cucumber, it won't continue to develop unless it's pollinated. Male flowers are generally the first to appear and they do so in greater numbers than the female flowers. Male flowers don't have a miniature fruit at the base of the blossom. Once you have some female flowers, you can try your hand at pollination.

Pollination Adaptations

Children are often excited by the concept that the primary "purpose" in the life of a flower is to become pollinated. All flowers have adaptations to assure that they achieve this purpose. Features such as bold colors or markings, convenient size or shape, or specific fragrance attract bees and other pollinators. As these creatures move from blossom to blossom, foraging for the sweet flower nectar and pollen that serve as food, they inadvertently transfer pollen. Other plants, such as grass and many trees, have small, light, inconspicuous flowers that are easily pollinated by wind and rain.

Have your students study flowers from the schoolyard, from home, and from the classroom garden. Use magnifying glasses to examine them and try to identify some of the flower parts. You can use the Flower Power diagram in Appendix C to help with identification, although not all flowers will possess all the parts shown. Feel some stigmas to see if they are sticky and have children guess why this might be. Ask students to describe flower characteristics that aid pollination.

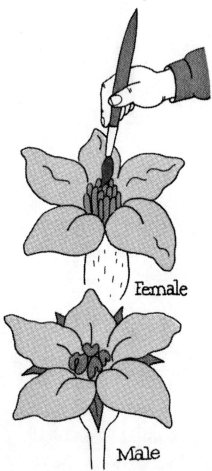

Female

Male

Using a small paintbrush, carefully collect the yellow pollen grains from the tip of the stamen (the anther) on the male flower, and gently touch the brush to the tip of the pistil (stigma) of the female flower. As long as some of the yellow pollen is transferred to the female, you're likely to achieve pollination. Female flowers that have not been pollinated will die.

Preparing for Vacation

After carefully tending your indoor school garden for weeks or months, you may find yourself worrying about having to leave it for an extended time because of a school vacation. Some teachers avoid this problem altogether by planning the calendar so garden projects end just before a vacation and new ones begin afterwards. Others choose to maintain plants through a vacation.

The more attention plants get during a vacation, the more likely they'll survive and thrive. If possible, arrange to check on the plants a couple of times during vacation, or consider enlisting extra help from your custodian or fellow teachers to decrease the workload. If this isn't possible, take the simple steps noted below to keep your plants alive for a week or more with little or no care. **The most important step is to make sure the soil around your plants stays moist.** Here is what you can do to prevent a drought in your indoor garden:

1. **If you have perlite in the base of your garden, add water to the tray until it nearly touches your pots.** (Two or three gallons should be plenty.) This water will evaporate during the vacation, keeping the humidity in your garden high. High humidity reduces water loss from your plants.

   If you are using capillary matting on top of trays as illustrated on page 28, fill the trays with water, moisten the matting, and dip the ends of the mats in the water to act as a wick. Water will be drawn up continually, providing humidity for the plants.

   If you are using matting directly on the plastic liner, fill a large container with water and wet your capillary matting wick and fabric. Place one end of the wick in the reservoir and the other end under the matting, ensuring good contact with the mat. If you have room, leave the reservoir inside the enclosed GrowLab. If you must leave it outside, cover the reservoir to reduce evaporation.

   If you are using moisture grids in trays, add water to the tray until it reaches the top of the grid.

2. **Completely cover your light garden with a plastic tent.** Sealing the unit in this way will prevent moisture from escaping, forming what amounts to a large terrarium. Make sure the covering is tucked inside the base, otherwise condensation will drip outside.

   Cover plants with clear plastic bags if you don't have a GrowLab or if you have large, rapidly growing plants that are in danger of using all the moisture in their soil during vacation. Pull a bag over each plant and tuck the bag opening into the top of the pot. Moisture that condenses will run back into the pot, continuing to water the plant. Support the bag inside with sticks so the bag doesn't touch leaves. Don't leave the plant in strong sunlight or it will be damaged.

3. **Reduce the number of hours your lights are on.** Although fluorescent and LED lights produce little heat, they do produce some, and the longer they're on, the more water the plants will use for growth. Plants can easily get by on ten hours of light each day for short periods.

4. **If you are using a heating cable or mat, don't leave it plugged in.** The heat would speed evaporation of water from the base and pots. An exception to this is if there is a danger of temperatures dropping very low during vacation. Leave the cable on in these circumstances after checking with the custodian regarding safety precautions. If you must leave a heating cable on, you'll need to find a reliable person to come in and water your plants every few days.

5. **If you have someone come in to water your plants,** make sure that person is reliable, will come in once or twice a week, knows what to do, and will seal up the covering again afterward.

6. **When you return, uncover the plants and check carefully for signs of insect or disease problems,** which can develop easily in still, warm, humid conditions. Check immediately so you can take action if necessary. If the soil and air are very damp after having been covered, remove the tent until they dry out a bit.

Caution

When covering your garden, be sure to attach the covering inside the frame on the side of the unit where electrical components are mounted. If you do not have a framework for your plant stand, do not drape anything directly over the light fixtures.

Chapter 5

Tackling Pests and Other Problems

A real advantage of indoor school gardening is that you can grow crops without having to protect them from most of their natural enemies. For instance, we don't find Mexican bean beetles, tomato hornworms, cucumber beetles, or woodchucks in our indoor gardens. Unfortunately some pests, and a number of diseases, can thrive in the warm, moist, predator-free environment the indoor garden provides. Don't be concerned that the appearance of pests and diseases will spell the end of your garden. Even insect-laden plants can produce a crop, and can certainly lend another dimension to your lessons! Armed with the information in this chapter, you and your students can address problems that do arise.

Prevention: The Best Medicine

The most important means of avoiding disease and pest problems is to prevent them from becoming established. This means being vigilant, providing conditions for healthy plant growth (healthy plants are the best defense against such problems), and practicing strict classroom garden hygiene as described below.

Pay attention. Ask the children to look carefully at their plants at least once a week. Take the pots out of the garden, lift them up, get a good look at the soil, and especially the underside of leaves — a favorite spot for pests. There are always students who love to be detectives in search of pest or disease clues. A magnifying glass is a useful and exciting tool for this job.

Don't wait if you notice a problem developing. Take action immediately before the problem has a chance to become established and spread to other plants.

Don't introduce houseplants with disease or insect problems to your garden — this will only invite trouble. If you decide to bring in houseplants, reduce the risk by inspecting them carefully. It's also wise to quarantine and monitor newcomers in a different part of the room for a few weeks.

Remove damaged, diseased, or weakened plant material regularly from the indoor garden. These materials attract insects and provide conditions for disease to develop.

Maintain good air circulation within the garden. Diseases can thrive in a stagnant environment, but will be less likely to do so if there is good air movement. Your students' daily movement around the classroom garden will provide some air circulation. If you're using a covered light garden, lift up the covering if conditions are too humid. Don't overcrowd plants. Thin plants when they are young to ensure good air circulation.

Disinfect your equipment. Make a solution of 1/2 cup chlorine bleach in 1 gallon of water. Use it to wash any pots you'll reuse. Rinse the pots in clear water to remove bleach residue. At the end of every year, replace the base material of your garden, or clean it with a bleach solution and rinse well.

Always use clean potting mix. Reusing potting mix, unless you have pasteurized it, invites trouble. Commercial soilless mixes are already sterile. If you have accumulated used growing mix in which healthy plants grew, you can reuse it for repotting large, well-established plants, but don't reuse it for young, fragile ones. A compost pile that heats up to 160°F is the best place for this used soil, because the heat will kill any harmful organisms.

If you have added garden soil or compost to your mix, you can pasteurize it by baking it in a covered container in a 180°F oven for thirty to forty minutes. As we've stated earlier in the book, it's a smelly process.

Fertilize properly. Read the directions on your fertilizer carefully. Too much fertilizer can cause lush, potentially weak growth that is extremely susceptible to attack. Aphids, in particular, are attracted to foliage with high levels of nitrogen. Too little fertilizer can also stress the plants.

Use good watering practices. Watering too often deprives the roots of air and promotes rot. Not watering enough stresses the plants and makes them more susceptible to disease and insects. When you plant seeds, make sure your potting mix isn't so moist that you can wring water out of it, since algae and fungi will thrive in these conditions. When you water, avoid splashing or wetting the leaves for the same reason.

Avoid too much moisture on foliage. Try to apply water to the soil and avoid wetting the leaves all together. If you must mist plants, don't touch them while the leaves are wet to avoid spreading water-borne diseases.

Environmental Problems

Even when you implement careful prevention techniques, pest or disease problems can develop. When you notice a problem, what should you do?

Sometimes symptoms that are misconstrued as signs of pest or disease problems are actually the result of poor management or other problems. First, determine if the cause is from environmental conditions, such as the location of the garden or positioning of the lights, or if it's from maintenance practices, like crowding the plants or watering too much. For instance, if your plants are stunted, yellowing, or otherwise abnormal looking, it may be from over- or underwatering or because container drainage holes are plugged up. Dry and scorched leaves may be the result of placing plants too close to the lights.

Before assuming that your plants are diseased, assess whether you can solve the problem by adjusting basic care or the environment of your garden. Review information in Tables 5 and 6, and study Table 7 (page 59). As you can see, similar symptoms can result from various causes. In exploring the cause of the trouble, consider all the potential sources: environmental conditions, location of the garden, and your own maintenance practices.

Pest Problems

If your class detectives do turn up evidence of pests in your garden, use the following information to help identify and control them. (See page 60 for detailed descriptions of the pest controls recommended here.) If none of these descriptions match your pest, check your local or state Cooperative Extension Web site for additional information.

Aphid
¹⁄₁₀" Long

Aphids are soft-bodied insects with or without wings. Both types are quite visible because they generally appear in clusters on the undersides of leaves, on stems, shoot tips, and flower buds. They may be pale green, grey, white, tan, or black.

Damage: During an infestation, leaves and shoot tips curl and turn yellow, and the plant will be generally weak. Aphids, like many insects, make a plant more susceptible to disease. They also transmit certain diseases.

Control: Often you can keep aphids in check by regularly washing infested plants with a strong spray of water. You can also use a soap spray. Although these treatments probably won't eliminate aphids from your plants entirely, they will reduce the population. Once aphids have found your plants, you'll need to remain watchful and respond quickly to reinfestations.

Whiteflies are very small (1/6 inch) white, winged insects found primarily on the undersides of leaves. When you disturb an infested plant, these pests rise in a cloud.

Damage: Unless there is a large infestation, whiteflies cause little direct damage to a plant, but their presence may lead to disease.

Control: Soap sprays are most effective against whitefly larvae; adults fly away and return when the treatment is complete. Spray every three to five days to keep up with the rapidly developing young. Since whiteflies are attracted to the color yellow, gardeners hang yellow cardboard covered with a sticky substance, such as 90-weight oil, to trap them.

Mealybugs are tan, soft-bodied insects covered with white, cottony fluff. They are most often found on the undersides of leaves and at the joints of stems.

Damage: An infestation of mealybugs will weaken a plant and may lead to disease.

Control: Because of their waxy coating and tenacity, you'll need to spray mealybugs with a solution of rubbing alcohol and water.

Spider Mites are tiny, reddish, barely visible dust specks. They first appear on the undersides of leaves but they quickly spread to other parts. In heavy infestations, you'll see their silky webbing over the leaves. (Yes, they really are members of the spider family!)

Damage: Spider mite feeding causes stippling (tiny spots of dead tissue), bleaching, and curling of leaves; serious infestations cause leaves to drop.

Control: Mites thrive in dry conditions, so provide plants with adequate moisture and periodically wash leaves with a stream of water.

Soil Insects, such as fungus gnats, may fly around your plants. They are most often a problem when you use garden soil or compost in a potting mix.

Damage: These insects are not usually harmful (although large infestations of fungus gnat larvae in soil can cause some damage to plant roots), but may be indicative of other problems. They thrive where humidity is high and are found near rotting organic matter.

Control: Water judiciously to avoid waterlogged soil and excessive humidity. For severe infestations, remove plants from their current pots, carefully rinse old soil from roots, and replant in new soil. Dispose of old soil in a compost pile or trashcan.

Rodents are sometimes attracted to soil and seedlings.

Control: Set traps out of reach of children, and warn them of the presence of traps. If your school building already has an established rodent problem, call upon your principal and custodian to handle it.

Pest Controls

We recommend soap spray and rubbing alcohol as the primary measures for controlling many indoor pests.

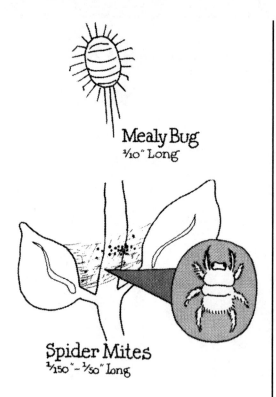

Mealy Bug
1/10" Long

Spider Mites
1/150" – 1/50" Long

Soap Spray

Soap Sprays are safe for use on food plants and are usually effective in controlling a number of plant pests including aphids, whiteflies, and spider mites. Not all soaps are equally suited to this task. Some can be caustic to your plants and all can be harmful if used in too concentrated a solution. Use either gentle dishwashing soaps (not detergents) or commercial insecticidal soaps. Dilute dish soap at a rate of 1 to 2 tablespoons per gallon of water; mix insecticidal soap as directed by the product label.

Application: Spray the solution on the affected plants with a plant mister or small pressure sprayer, covering the foliage thoroughly, especially the undersides of leaves. You can also dip an entire plant in a container of soap solution. If you're unsure about the effect of applying a particular soap, test it on a single leaf or small section of a leaf and observe results. Watch carefully for reinfestaton and spray again in a few days if necessary.

Rubbing Alcohol is useful for controlling indoor pests such as mealybugs, but it can damage plants if applied improperly.

Application: If the infestation is small, apply to pests one at a time using a cotton swab. If pests are too numerous to treat individually, mix a half-and-half solution of water and rubbing alcohol and spray the affected parts with a mister. Since alcohol may harm certain plants, rinse plants immediately after the treatment with clear water.

Additional Pest Treatments

Even if your district or state government does not have a policy that prohibits the use of pesticides in your school or classroom, we strongly discourage their use. Many pesticides are persistent in the environment and toxic not only to specific pests, but also to beneficial insects, fish, animals, and humans. Pesticide use is regulated by state governments and the Environmental Protection Agency. You, the teacher, may therefore be liable for misuse and for any problems associated with use of pesticides in the classroom. Before you purchase such substances — even those labeled "organic" — contact your school principal and/or superintendent's office for advice.

Diseases and Algae

The best way to avoid disease problems is to provide ideal conditions — good air circulation, watering, and fertilizing practices — for your indoor garden and to practice strict garden hygiene. It's difficult to eradicate diseases once they become established, so prevention pays off! Refer to the information below to help determine if your plants have disease problems.

Powdery Mildew primarily affects cucumbers, zinnias, and possibly beans in an indoor garden. Leaves appear to be dusted with a white powder (fungal spores and mycelia). Serious infections cause leaves to turn brown and wither, and weakened plants die. This seldom happens in indoor gardens where infestations tend to be mild and mainly cosmetic.

Control: Unlike most other fungal diseases, powdery mildew thrives in dry as well as humid conditions. You can physically wipe "powder" from leaves, or rinse spores away with a hard spray of water.

Grey Mold appears as brown patches that eventually become covered with grey or brown fuzzy mold. It is commonly found on dead plant material in moist conditions, but it can migrate to healthy plants.

Control: Clean up dead plant debris. There's no control for affected plants. Remove and discard all affected materials to prevent further spread.

Damping Off is a fungal disease that causes seedlings to rot suddenly at the soil level and fall over (see illustration). It affects the seedlings of many vegetables and flower plants and may also prevent seeds from germinating.

Control: Prevent damping off by covering newly planted seeds with 1/8 inch of sphagnum peat moss. Remove and discard any affected plants and the soil around them. Discard or sterilize potting mix and containers in which affected plants were growing. Set up a fan near your garden to improve air circulation around seedlings.

Bean Mosaic is a viral disease carried by aphids and by seeds of infected plants. Infected bean leaves appear puckered and eventually turn yellow and die. The virus weakens plants and may interfere with fruiting.

Control: There is no control for viral diseases. Prevent viruses by keeping the aphid population in check. Remove and discard affected plants immediately (if you have only a few bean plants, you may want to keep them in order to observe the progress of the disease, since it won't affect other crops).

Fungi and Algae appear as fuzzy white, dry brown, or green (algae) growths on the soil or base material surface. Although they're not problems in themselves, they do indicate moist conditions and poor air circulation, which could lead to other problems.

Control: If you notice these growths, stir the soil or base material with a fork or your fingers once a week. Also, decrease humidity in the garden by uncovering it and increasing air circulation.

Algae is more likely to form on your base material in the presence of intense fluorescent light. If your growing unit is only partially filled, cover exposed portions of the base material with aluminum foil, heavy cardboard, or dark plastic sheets.

Botanical and synthetic pesticides are toxic substances. We strongly discourage their use in the classroom. You should not eat indoor food crops that have been treated with pesticides.

Don't confuse fungi and algae with the dry, crusty white buildup of fertilizer salts that may form on the soil surface if pots are not watered thoroughly. If you notice this dry, crusty buildup, loosen the soil with a fork and water thoroughly to flush out salts.

Environmental Causes of Poor Plant Health — Table 7

POSSIBLE CAUSES	FOLIAGE					GROWTH			FLOWERS		
	Wilted	All Leaves Dropped	Oldest Leaves Dropped	Yellowish Leaves	Tips Brown	Plant Died	New Leaves, Small	Spindly, Weak, Thin	No Blooms	Pale Color	Buds Dropped
Insufficient Light (impairs photosynthesis and flowering)			●	●		●	●	●	●	●	●
Light Scorch (plants too close to lights)				●	●						
High Temperature (especially at night, impairs growth and flowering)	●		●	●			●	●	●	●	●
Low Temperature	●					●					●
Overwatering or Poor Drainage (reduces soil aeration; roots die or nutrients can't be absorbed)	●	●	●	●	●	●	●	●		●	●
Lack of Water	●	●	●		●	●	●				●
Low Humidity (a danger particularly in winter)	●		●		●						●
Too Much Fertilizer (injures plant roots and becomes toxic to plant)	●	●	●	●	●	●	●				●
Lack of Fertilizer			●	●	●		●	●		●	●
Compacted or Heavy Soil (reduces root growth and activity)	●		●	●		●	●	●		●	●
Lack of Pollination											●

Chapter 6

Equipment Care and Maintenance

Proper care and maintenance can extend the life of your indoor gardening equipment. This chapter describes recommended cleaning and storage procedures to ensure that your GrowLab remains a useful educational tool for many years. You'll also find troubleshooting information with answers to the most common technical problems reported by teachers.

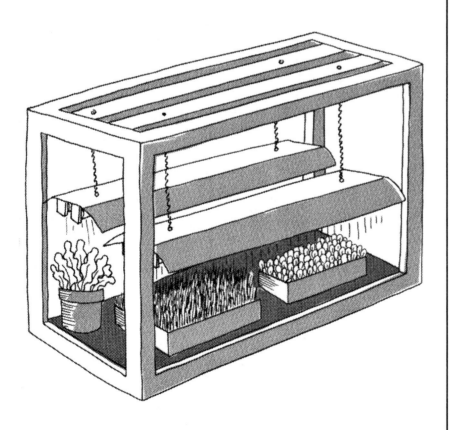

Cleaning and Storing Equipment

It pays to take care of your classroom garden at the end of the school year, whether it will be spending the summer in your classroom, stored away in a supply closet, or transported to a central storage area. Proper care can help to avoid summer damage, loss, or theft. Cleaning and storing your GrowLab as described below should ensure that it remains safe and sound over the summer months, and that it will be complete and ready for action come fall.

1. **Discard all used soil mix (compost it if possible) and clean pots and trays with a solution of 1/2 cup bleach to 1 gallon of water.**

2. **Remove the capillary mat, moisture grids, or perlite from the base of the unit.** Wash capillary matting or moisture grids thoroughly in a solution of 1/2 cup bleach per gallon of warm sudsy water. Rinse well and allow them to air dry before storing them. Perlite is fairly inexpensive, so if you used a perlite base you may choose to discard it at the end of the year (you can compost it, too); however, if you would rather reuse it, you can clean it. Soak perlite for an hour in the same bleach solution described above, then rinse it well in clear water, and spread it out on sheets of plastic to air dry for two days. When completely dry, store it in a trash bag or covered container.

3. **Clean the base of a homemade indoor garden using the same proportion of bleach solution used for the base material.** Clean the aluminum frame of a prefabricated GrowLab with soap and water and dry the frame well before storing it. If the base is lined with plastic, check for holes, repair them with duct tape, then store the plastic.

4. **Unplug the lights and clean the tubes.** Wipe the tubes with a damp cloth. You'll want to do this again before you reinstall lights in the fall, since dust can significantly cut down on the light that reaches your plants. Reinsert the tubes into the fixtures or wrap tubes individually in several thicknesses of newspaper and store them in a safe place. Wide-spectrum or full-spectrum bulbs will retain their useful life for two to three years under normal use. Cool white bulbs should be replaced annually.

5. **Take down the light fixtures if they are on chains.** Wrap up their cords. Place the fixtures tube side up in the base of the GrowLab to protect them from breakage during moving.

6. **Unplug the timer and store it out of sight in a bag or box.**

7. **Cover the whole GrowLab with paper or plastic to keep out dust.**

Troubleshooting

The GrowLab is designed to be as trouble-free as possible so teachers can concentrate on teaching. However, sometimes equipment does malfunction. The following paragraphs detail common problems you may experience to help you troubleshoot and find possible solutions. If you feel uneasy about diagnosing problems, consult with your custodian or an experienced electrician. Also, be sure to read Appendix D for details on the GrowLab electrical components.

Caution

Take extra care when using bleach solution around children.

Problem: None of your light fixtures work.

Possible Solutions: First check to make sure that your main plug is plugged into a functioning wall outlet. Check the outlet by plugging in something you know to be in working order.

Check to see that your timer is operating (see below).

Check your ground fault circuit interruptor (see below).

If you have checked all of the above and none of your lights are working, you should consult an electrician for assistance. The problem must be in the main cord or outlet box.

Problem: Lights come on but are dim or flickering.

Possible Solutions: Wait until the room heats up. Temperatures below 45°F may affect light operation.

Make sure that the tubes are properly installed. A loose tube can cause flickering or total failure of both tubes in the fixture. This kind of problem is the source of most lighting failures.

At both ends of each fixture there are terminals (usually made of plastic), and the tubes are installed between them. In each terminal is a slot into which the pins on the tube are inserted. After the tube is inserted in both terminals, twist it a quarter turn until it is seated correctly and is firm. When a tube is correctly seated, you'll see a small bump, groove, or mark at each end of the tube. This mark should line up with the slot into which you inserted the pins (facing straight down). Always remember to turn off or unplug lights before adjusting tubes or removing light covers.

If the tubes are properly installed and still aren't working, check to see if they are still usable. Remove the non-functioning tube and place it in a fixture that you know to be working. If the tube does not work there either, the tube needs to be replaced. If it does work in the new fixture, the problem is probably inside the original light fixture.

Check inside the light fixture. This should be done by someone with some experience with electrical wiring. You can take off most covers by removing screws or clips.

Once inside, look for loose wires. Check where the wires are inserted into the terminals and where they are connected to each other and to the power cord. Gently tug on them. If you find a loose one, try to reconnect it by pushing it into the appropriate terminal or by reconnecting it in the wire nut (the little conical cap that screws over wire ends and makes them connect).

If none of this helps, the problem may be with the ballast in your light. Unless you can find an electrician who will solve the problem, you should replace the fixture.

Problem: Your timer isn't working but the electricity is on.

Possible Solutions: Thoroughly read the directions that came with the timer. Check to see that the timer setting pieces are in the correct place and that the timer is properly set.

Check the override switch on the timer.

Always turn off or unplug lights before adjusting tubes or removing light covers.

GFCI

Make sure that your lights are plugged into the timer outlet. If they aren't plugged directly into the timer (or into a multi-outlet strip connected to the timer), it will seem as though your timer isn't working.

If it is not working at all, check the ground fault circuit interruptor.

Problem: Ground fault circuit interruptor (GFCI) not working or constantly tripping. (Please note that pre-fabricated GrowLabs do not include a ground fault circuit interrupter.)

Possible Solutions: If the timer is no longer humming, check the GFCI to see if it has been tripped off. If the "T" button is pushed in, leaving a red bar showing on the "R" button, the GFCI has been tripped for some reason. Press the reset button to resume power. If there is a real electrical problem, the GFCI will trip off again for safety. Chances are, however, the unit will resume operation.

If the GFCI trips frequently, make sure the plastic covering your GrowLab does not enclose the ground fault circuit interruptor. GFCI units are very sensitive devices that may be tripped off by humidity. Lift part of the plastic to allow for increased air circulation.

If the timer continues to trip, check all wire connections and look for frays. A short circuit is probably occurring.

Problem: Heating cable isn't working.

Possible Solutions: Check the plug connections to see if it is properly attached. This is particularly important if you installed a plug from a kit.

Check to see if the heating cable is broken. This generally happens when the cable is not well secured to the base of the growing unit. If the heating cable crosses itself the resulting heat melts the insulation and causes the cable to short and break. Close examination of the cable will reveal this condition. Never use a damaged heating cable. A heating cable cannot be repaired. Replace it or give it up entirely, since it's not critical to the operations of the classroom garden unless your building is extremely cold for extended periods.

Appendix A

Indoor Garden Growers' Guide

The classroom garden Growers' Guide is a general reference that provides information on growing and harvesting vegetables, flowers, and herbs in your classroom. This guide suggests specific, well-suited varieties. If you follow the guidelines in the Growers' Guide table, the growing and harvest information, and the management information in the main text, you should be rewarded with a successful garden.

We encourage you to use this guide as a springboard. Read through other gardening references for additional information and experiment on your own with new crops, varieties, and growing techniques.

Growing and Harvesting Vegetables

The following list provides information about vegetables that can be successfully grown in an indoor garden. It does not include corn and potatoes, or heading crops such as cabbage, cauliflower, and head lettuce, because these vegetables won't grow to maturity indoors. However, you can start seedlings of any crops that transplant well to outdoor gardens.

Beans — Choose bush beans over pole beans, since most will grow only to 18 inches and will remain compact enough to benefit from the lights. If you are gardening on the windowsill, try growing pole beans and training them to climb up strings by the windows.

Harvest: Harvest beans when the pods are full but before the outline of the enclosed seed shows. Continue to harvest as pods mature to encourage more pods to form. You should be able to pick beans for several weeks.

Beets — Beets are easy to grow indoors, but tend to grow more slowly and yield smaller roots than those grown in outdoor gardens.

Harvest: Beet greens are best harvested and eaten when young and tender. They are rich in vitamins and minerals, and are delicious cooked or raw in salads. Leave some greens to continue supplying food to the roots. Harvest roots, which you can feel under the soil with your fingers, when they are just over 1 inch in diameter.

Carrots — Carrots, like beets, are easy to grow indoors, but grow rather slowly. The most helpful thing you can do to encourage a good crop is to thin seedlings properly, since crowding hinders healthy root growth. If the carrot shoulders push out of the soil, cover them with more soil to prevent the exposed parts from becoming dry and green.

Harvest: Pull carrots when they are 1/4 to 1/2 inch in diameter.

Chinese Cabbage (Bok Choi, Pak Choi) — This is a nonheading type of Chinese cabbage with thick, celery-like midribs and tender, dark green leaves that grows to about 16 inches. The stems and leaves are good raw in salads or cooked.

Harvest: Pick young leaves to eat raw and use larger leaves and stems for cooking.

Collards — Collards have coarse cabbage-like leaves. Unlike other members of the cabbage family (cabbage, broccoli, and cauliflower), collard plants do not form heads, so they grow well under lights.

Harvest: Pick young greens for eating raw in salads; harvest older leaves for hot dishes. If you pick just the leaves and leave the main stem, the stem should produce another crop.

Cucumbers — Choose seed varieties labeled "compact" or "bush-type," though even these types can take up a lot of space. Cucumbers have separate male and female flowers. Male flowers will appear first and will greatly outnumber the female flowers. Once you have some of both, hand-pollinate them as described on page 53. Plant breeders have developed gynoecious (self-pollinating, all-female) cucumber varieties that do not require germination, so you might want to try them as well.

Harvest: Pick fruits when they reach the mature size described on the seed packet. Keep picking to encourage more fruit to form.

Eggplant — These warm-weather plants have deep root systems, but will produce fruit in containers indoors. Look for dwarf varieties when buying seed.

Harvest: Pick fruits when they reach the mature size described on the seed packet and the skin is glossy.

Lettuce — Looseleaf varieties grow best under lights. Heading types won't form heads indoors. Lettuce prefers cool temperatures and plenty of water. Keep soil moist to prevent leaves from becoming bitter.

Harvest: Pinch off or snip outer leaves as needed or cut whole plants at soil level for a larger harvest. If you leave the roots in the soil and keep fertilizing and watering them, they will produce another crop in about eight weeks. If lettuce is left growing for too long, particularly in hot temperatures, it will become bitter.

Mustard Greens — Mustard is a beautiful, vitamin-rich, green, leafy plant. Its appearance contrasts nicely with many of the other indoor garden crops and its sharp flavor will be a novelty for some students.

Harvest: Cut leaves when they are 4 inches or smaller for salad; cook larger leaves. If you leave a short piece of stem when cutting leaves, you can harvest again in about four weeks.

Onion Tops — An advantage of growing onions is that you can use any part of the plants at any time in their life cycle. We do not recommend growing onions to mature bulbs in the indoor garden because this takes so long. Bunching onions, grown for scallions, also have a long growing season and we don't recommend them, either. Instead, plant regular onion varieties from seeds or sets and harvest them as greens. Onion seeds generally do not remain viable for more than a year, so be sure to plant fresh seed each season.

Harvest: Snip tops during the young, tender green stage.

Parsley — This is a slow-growing crop, but it can produce a reasonable harvest in a single pot. Once sprouted, it is relatively trouble-free and can continue producing throughout the year. Soak seeds overnight in water before planting to stimulate germination.

Harvest: Snip sprigs as needed. As long as some foliage is left, the plant will continue to produce more leaves.

Peanuts — Although these may take up to five months to mature indoors under lights, they are beautiful plants and can be an exciting addition to the indoor garden. A couple of months after planting, bright orange/yellow, pea-like flowers will form. The small flowers that form lower on the plant are the ones that will be fertile. After self-fertilizing, they will bend downward and bury themselves. Add soil to the top of the pot to help bury them.

Harvest: Look periodically at the developing peanut under the surface. When mature, the kernels will look plump and will have the distinctive peanut texture with pronounced veins. If left too long, young peanuts

of some varieties will sprout and begin to grow new plants. Shell and toast the raw seeds. Warm a pan over low heat, add seeds, and stir constantly for ten to fifteen minutes. Sprinkle with salt and enjoy!

Peas

Peas — There are a number of short pea varieties that you can raise under lights. Peas require cool conditions; growth slows considerably when temperatures exceed 60°F. Unless your room is very hot, however, you should be able to get a small, token harvest indoors.

Harvest: Start picking when pods have swelled to an almost round shape. Don't let mature pods stay on the plant; this will cut down on your yields.

Peppers

Peppers — Although peppers are relatively slow to mature, they produce a nice crop of rather small fruits and provide an interesting addition to the indoor garden. They do require warm temperatures (between 65° and 80°F) at blossom time in order to produce fruit. If your room isn't consistently warm, we do not recommend that you grow them. Ornamental peppers, available in most seed catalogs and garden centers, are even slower to mature, but they make very nice gift plants. The tiny, colorful fruits are edible and very spicy.

Harvest: Clip peppers from stems as soon as they reach usable size (2 inches in diameter). You can also leave them on the plants until they turn their mature color (red, yellow, etc.).

Radishes

Radishes — Radishes give the quickest results of all indoor garden crops, producing a large number of roots in a single pot just four weeks after planting. Keep soil moist, thin the seedlings, and keep them close to the lights to promote good root development.

Harvest: Pick radishes when you see from the shoulders that they are the size of a small marble. They become woody when left in the soil for too long.

Strawberries (Alpine)

Strawberries (Alpine) — These are small strawberries, grown from seed, with a flavor reminiscent of wild strawberries. You can raise them as indoor plants or move them out to a garden or flower border. The seeds take quite a while to germinate, so make sure to keep them moist.

Harvest: Harvest berries as they ripen. Plants will bear small fruits over a period of several months.

Swiss Chard

Swiss Chard — This is a good indoor crop since you can use it raw or cooked, like spinach. Unlike spinach, Swiss chard grows well in warm indoor environments.

Harvest: Pick the outer leaves before they get tough, and new leaves will grow from the center. For a continued harvest, don't pick all of the leaves.

Tomatoes

Tomatoes — When buying tomato seed, look for designated container varieties, such as 'Tiny Tim'. You can stimulate more fruit production by carefully pinching back the little shoots (suckers) that grow between the main stems and the branches. You may need to stake tomato plants or tie the vines to the light garden frame for support.

Harvest: If you want to hasten the ripening process, try placing a very ripe apple in a pot of green tomatoes. (The ethylene gas produced by the ripening apple will stimulate tomatoes to turn red.) Although tomatoes will ripen off the vine, allowing them to ripen on the vine will provide best flavor and maximum production of vitamin C. Twist the fruit carefully from the stem when it's ready to pick.

Turnips — It's easy to grow turnips to a reasonable size indoors. Eat these white-fleshed roots raw or cooked. Young turnip greens are very nutritious, and like beet greens, are tasty when eaten raw or cooked.

Harvest: Harvest as you would carrots, when the roots are between 1 and 2 inches in diameter.

Key to Planting Chart Headings

Suggested Varieties — We recommend these varieties because they perform well indoors in containers. If you choose other varieties, keep in mind factors such as number of weeks to maturity, special cultural requirements, and, most importantly, size and growth habit. Because you need to keep the lights close to all the plants in your garden, look for compact, low-growing varieties. Fortunately, there are miniature types of many vegetables and flower plants. Seed catalogs and packets often indicate which varieties are specifically suited for container growing.

Days to Germination — This will give you an approximate idea of when to expect your seeds to germinate, given reasonable conditions. Room temperature, moisture levels, and a number of other factors affect germination.

Weeks to Maturity — Again, these are approximations of the number of weeks from planting until harvest.

Plants Per 6-inch Pot — We recommend this size pot. This column lists the number of plants that can be reasonably grown in each 6-inch diameter pot. Overcrowding in pots results in poor growth.

Plants Per Smaller Pot — Many teachers use small (3- or 4-inch pots) or 1/2-pint school milk cartons for planting, so we've included, for the vegetable crops, numbers of plants you can grow in these. Note: Many plants cannot be grown to maturity in such small pots.

Depth of Planting — Generally you should plant seeds at a depth three times their width. This column lists specific planting depths. Some of the annual flower crops listed require light to germinate or are too tiny to be buried under soil. A "0" appearing in this column indicates that you should plant seeds on top of the soil and press them down lightly with a smooth-surfaced object.

Low Light — You can grow many crops successfully on a windowsill or under only one or two light fixtures, but some will not produce well under these circumstances. Use this column to determine which crops will be more likely to thrive under lower light conditions.

Yield — The yields you can expect in an indoor garden are considerably less than you would expect outdoors, so for many crops we have included a rough idea of the amount that you can expect to harvest from each 6-inch pot.

Nutrients — This column lists the vitamins and minerals each vegetable provides in substantial amounts.

note:

In the "**Days to germination**" column at right, soak seeds designated with an asterisk in water for 24 hours before planting to stimulate germination.

Vegetable Planting Chart

Crop	Varieties	Days to Germination	Weeks to Maturity	Plants Per 6" Pot
BEANS	Contender Bush Blue Lake	4-8	8-9	1-2
BEETS	Early Wonder Cylindra Mini-Ball Ruby Queen	5-12*	9-12	4-5
CARROTS	Little Finger Short 'n Sweet Baby Finger Nantes Thumbelina	8-16	10-11	4-6
CHINESE CABBAGE (nonheading)	Mei Quing Choi Joy Choi	5-8	9-12	1
COLLARDS	Vates	4-6	11	1-2
CUCUMBERS	Lemon Salad Bush Suyo Fanfare	5-10	9	1
EGGPLANT	Little Fingers Bambino Ichiban Green Goddess	20+	12+	1
LETTUCE	Tom Thumb Black Seeded Simpson Salad Bowl Red Salad Bowl Oak Leaf	4-8	7-8	4
MUSTARD GREENS	Green Wave Tendergreen	4-10	6-8	1-2
ONION TOPS	Southport Yellow Globe White Sweet Spanish	7-14	6-8	12+
PARSLEY	Extra Curled Dwarf Italian (flat)	10-20*	8-10	4-6
PEANUTS	Early Spanish	7-14	20+	1
PEAS	Green Arrow Laxton's Progress	5-10	8-10	1-2
PEPPERS	Ace Sweet Red Cherry	8-14	9-12	1
RADISHES	Cherry Belle Early Scarlet Globe Easter Egg French Breakfast	3-5	4-5	6-8
STRAWBERRIES	(Alpine)	20	12+	2
TOMATOES	Tiny Tim Patio Hybrid Pixie Hybrid Red Robin	6-10	10-12+	1-2
TURNIPS	Purple White Top Globe Tokyo Cross	3-7	6-8	4
SWISS CHARD	Fordhook Giant Bright Lights	7-14	8-10	1-2

Plants Per Smaller Pot	Depth (Inches)	Low Light	Yield (Approx.)	Nutrients
–	1-1$\frac{1}{2}$	no	6-10 per plant	Protein; Vitamins B, C
2	$\frac{1}{2}$	yes	1"-1$\frac{1}{2}$" diameter roots	Greens high in Vitamins A, C; iron; calcium
–	$\frac{1}{2}$	yes	$\frac{1}{2}$" diameter, 2"-long roots	Vitamin A
–	$\frac{1}{2}$	yes	2 cuttings	Vitamins A, C; calcium
–	$\frac{1}{4}$-$\frac{1}{2}$	yes	2 cuttings	Vitamins A, C; calcium
–	$\frac{1}{2}$-1	no	1-3 6" cukes per plant	small amount of Vitamin C
–	$\frac{1}{4}$-$\frac{1}{2}$	no	1-2 small fruits per plant	small amounts of Vitamin C; potassium
1-2	$\frac{1}{4}$-$\frac{1}{2}$	yes	4 small plants	Vitamin A; potassium; calcium
1	$\frac{1}{4}$-$\frac{1}{2}$	yes	2 cuttings of 6" leaves	Vitamins A, C, Bs; calcium; iron
6+	$\frac{1}{2}$	yes	continuous cuttings	potassium
1-2	$\frac{1}{4}$-$\frac{1}{2}$	yes	continuous cuttings	Vitamins A, C
–	1$\frac{1}{2}$	no	3-6 per plant	protein, Vitamin B
–	2	no	4-6 pods per plant	protein; Vitamins B_1, C; iron
–	$\frac{1}{4}$-$\frac{1}{2}$	no	2 small fruits per plant	Vitamins A, C
3	$\frac{1}{4}$-$\frac{1}{2}$	yes	$\frac{1}{2}$"-1" diameter roots	Vitamin C
1	$\frac{1}{8}$	yes	4-8 tiny berries	Vitamin C; iron
–	$\frac{1}{4}$-$\frac{1}{2}$	yes	6-15 small fruits per plant	Vitamins A, C; potassium
1-2	$\frac{1}{4}$-$\frac{1}{2}$	yes	1"-2" diameter roots	Greens high in calcium; Vitamins A, C; iron
–	$\frac{1}{2}$	yes	continuous cuttings	Vitamin A; calcium; iron

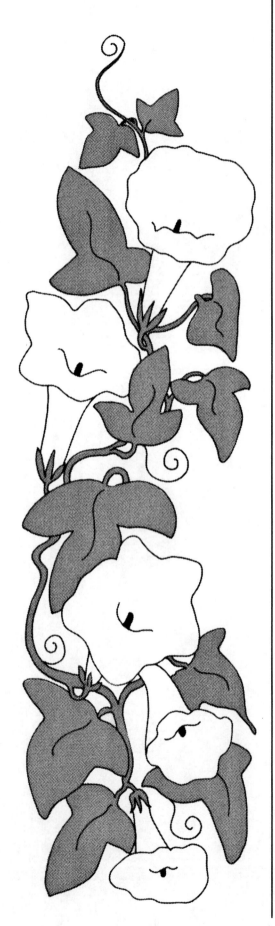

Growing Flowers

You can grow many annual garden flowers from seed to brighten the classroom. This section provides basic cultural information and suggested varieties. As with vegetables, when choosing varieties of annual flowers for indoors, look for relatively low-growing or dwarf types.

Ageratums — Ageratums are low-growing plants, so nearly any variety will do. The flowers are compact, dense, woolly looking blue, pink, or white puffballs.

Alyssum — Alyssum is another low-growing border plant that comes in a variety of cool colors from white to deep purple. Delicate, honey-scented flowers take a while to bloom, but will bloom for a long time.

Coleus — This attractive plant is grown for its brightly colored variegated leaves. Although you can easily propagate coleus from stem cuttings, it's fun to start these plants from seed. Press the tiny seeds into place on your growing medium and mist carefully. Pinch back the main stems to encourage branching and bushy growth. To keep leaves looking their best, pinch off the small blue flowers as they develop.

Impatiens — Impatiens are among the most difficult flowers on this list to grow from seed, but they are easy to grow from cuttings. Seeds are extremely small and the seedlings are often susceptible to damping off. Nonetheless, their succulent stems and colorful flowers earn them a place on this list.

Marigolds — Dwarf marigolds are a great addition to the indoor garden. Once the seeds germinate, the plants grow well and produce a profusion of blossoms ranging from almost red to pale yellow. Pinch back main stems to encourage branching.

Morning Glories — Although these plants twine and vine so much that you can't grow them for long in a light garden, the trumpet-shaped blue flowers add a nice accent to the gardening classroom when you grow them up strings near the window.

Nasturtiums — These plants serve a double purpose in your garden: They produce brightly colored flowers, ranging from cream to dark red, and rounded leaves, all of which are edible. The lovely flowers and peppery-flavored leaves add zip to garden salads.

Petunias — Petunia seeds are very fine and difficult to work with. Scatter them on top of the soil mix and mist them until they germinate. These sturdy flowers will bloom for a long time in the classroom or outside.

Snapdragons — These colorful, dragon-like flowers add a unique touch to classroom gardens. Choose dwarf varieties if you plan to keep them under lights. If your flowers are sparse, your indoor garden may be too warm for their liking.

Zinnias — Zinnias are often the bright stars of indoor gardens. A dwarf mix will yield a wide range of colors over a long period. Seeds are large and easy to handle. Their main disadvantage is their susceptibility to fungus problems.

You can bring many other garden annuals to flower in the indoor garden, including those listed below. We encourage you to experiment.

asters (Color Carpet)   geranium
begonias (fibrous dwarf)   portulaca
celosia   primula
creeping phlox   salvia
dianthus (Snowfire)   verbena

You may find that certain plants produce lovely foliage and even buds, but fail to flower. This may have to do with the amount of light they receive. Some species are short-day plants, meaning that they flower when they receive about ten hours of daylight. Since you will be leaving the lights in your garden on for fourteen to sixteen hours, short-day flowers may not bloom under these conditions. Some flowers also blossom best in cool conditions, and your environment may be too warm.

Perennials — You can start many perennial flowers in an indoor garden for transplanting outdoors the following year. Ask children to bring in dried seeds of various wild or cultivated perennials and experiment to see if you can germinate and grow them. Some of the easiest perennials to grow include: black-eyed Susan, Shasta daisy, coral bells, baby's breath, lupine, poppy, and foxglove.

Flower Planting Chart

Crop	Varieties	Days to Germination	Weeks to Maturity	Plants Per 6" Pot	Depth* (Inches)
AGERATUM	Blue Mink Blue Danube	5-10	9	4-6	0
ALYSSUM	Easter Basket Mix Carpet of Snow	5-14	10-12	6-8	0
COLEUS	Rainbow	10-14	–	4-6	0
DIANTHUS	Snowfire	10-14	9	4-6	1/8
IMPATIENS	Blitz Super Elfin	10-20	9	4-6	0
MARIGOLD	Petite Mix Inca Gold	5-7	11	4-6	1/8
MORNING GLORY	Heavenly Blue	5-7	6-8	3-4	1/4
NASTURTIUM	Dwarf Jewel	7-14	8-10	1-2	1/2
PETUNIA	–	10	10-12	3-4	0
SNAPDRAGON	Floral Carpet	10-15	10	3-4	1/8
ZINNIA	Thumbelina	5-7	10	4-6	1/8

note:

*Some seeds require light to germinate or are too tiny to be buried under soil. A "0" in the "Depth" column at left indicates that you should plant these seeds on top of the soil, pressing down lightly on them with a smooth surface. Do not bury them.

Growing Herbs

Herbs add a fragrant dimension to the indoor garden. In addition to their culinary uses, many are ideal for craft projects such as wreaths, flavored vinegars, sachets, and the like. You can use herbs at all stages of growth and they do well under lights or on a windowsill. Most herbs grow more slowly than vegetable plants.

You can grow all of the herbs listed in the Herb Planting Chart from seed or from plants purchased at a nursery. When purchasing seed, look for dwarf or compact varieties.

Herb Planting Chart

Herb	Type	Days to Germination	Plants Per 6" Pot	Planting Depth (Inches)
BASIL	annual	7-10	2-3	1/8
CATNIP	perennial	5-14	3-4	1/8
CORIANDER/CILANTRO	annual	10-12	3	1/2
CHIVES	perennial	5-14	20-30	1/4
DILL	annual	5-10	3-4	1/4
MARJORAM	perennial	10-16	2-4	1/8
SPEARMINT	perennial	10-16	3-4	1/8
OREGANO	perennial	8-14	2-4	1/8
PARSLEY	biennial	10-20	4-6	1/4 - 1/2
SAGE	perennial	14-21	3-4	1/4
SUMMER SAVORY	annual	14-21	1-2	1/2
THYME	perennial	20-30	4-6	1/8

note:

Some of the herbs listed as perennials may be grown as annuals, depending on your region's growing conditions and the plant variety.

Another way to propagate perennial herbs is to pot up divisions. Make divisions by cutting pieces, roots and all, from existing plant clumps.

Although many herb plants can grow quite large if left to their own devices, you can control them and encourage bushy growth by pinching back new top growth periodically. (Use the trimmings in recipes.) Also pinch back developing flower buds to encourage the growth of flavorful foliage.

Appendix B

Special Projects for Indoor Gardens

Y ou can do much more than grow vegetables, flowers, and herbs from seed in your GrowLab. Many teachers use their indoor gardens for special projects that enhance plant science investigations and help expand on concepts such as vegetative propagation (growing new plants from parts of old plants), plant adaptations, and ecosystems.

Some of these projects result in houseplants, colorful bulbs, or thriving terrariums that students can take home, sell to support the garden program, or keep in the classroom for more investigations — and pure enjoyment.

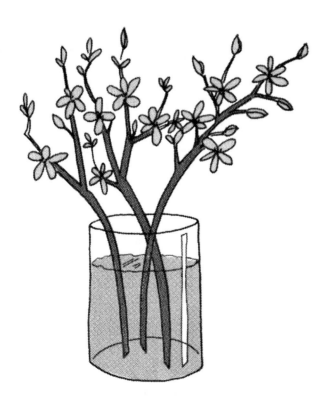

figure A

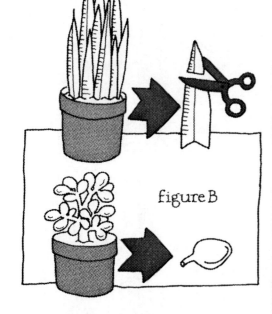

figure B

figure C

note:

Many people root cuttings in water. Although some plants will develop many roots with this method, the roots often have fewer root hairs, are more brittle, and transplant poorly. Your class can conduct an experiment comparing the growth of cuttings rooted in water and other rooting mixes.

Houseplant Cuttings

Rooting plant cuttings is an easy way to increase your collection quickly, and to teach about vegetative propagation. Many common houseplants root nicely in a light garden or on a windowsill. You can repot these new plants for your classroom or send them home with the children. Here's a list of houseplants we recommend for this purpose.

Stem Cuttings	Leaf Cuttings	Plantlets
impatiens	snake plant	aloe
coleus	jade plant	spider plant
chrysanthemum	begonia	piggyback plant
African violet	African violet	
geranium		
philodendron		
wandering jew		
Swedish ivy		

How to Root Cuttings

1. **Water plants well the day before taking cuttings.** This reduces dehydration after cutting.

2. **You can root many cuttings in one container to save space and soilless mix.** Repot them once the cuttings have rooted. Use your soilless mix (or a mixture made from equal volumes of perlite and vermiculite) as a rooting medium. Make sure the mix is moist, but not soaking wet, or your cuttings will rot.

3. **Fill the container with mix, gently firm it in place, and make small holes** (1/2 inch to 1 inch deep) **with your finger or pencil,** spaced as close as 2 inches apart.

4. **Next, take cuttings as described below.** Be sure to hold a cutting by the leaf, not by the stem. If a leaf is damaged, a new one can grow, but a damaged stem can kill a plant.

   Stem cuttings — Take cuttings from newer, faster-growing stems by snipping with scissors just below the third or fourth pair of leaves. Strip off the lower pair of leaves (roots will probably grow from here) leaving two to three sets of healthy leaves above (see figure A).

   Leaf cuttings — Cut a leaf with its stem (petiole). If you're propagating a snake plant, cut a two-inch section from the middle of the leaf (see figure B). Plant as described in Step 5.

   Plantlets — Some plants grow tiny plantlets at the end of runners (spider plant), or at the base of the stem of the mother plant (aloe). Carefully cut these offshoots from the mother plant (see figure C) and treat them as described below.

5. **Carefully place the cutting into the hole and firm the soil around it.** You can dip the cutting in a commercial rooting hormone (available at most garden centers) to speed rooting and prevent stem rot. It's not necessary to use rooting hormone, but it offers an opportunity for students to design experiments (like the one described in the Classrooom Profile on page 79) to test its effectiveness.

6. **Place individual containers inside plastic bags** and tie each one closed

to retain moisture for rooting. Use stakes or plant labels to keep the plastic from touching the leaves.

7. **Place the containers under lights in a warm area.** A light garden offers a perfect environment for rooting. If you don't have a GrowLab or other light setup, place containers in a warm, bright area, but avoid direct sunlight, which can result in a "greenhouse effect" that can cook your cuttings!

8. **Check the containers occasionally to ensure that the soilless mix is moist.** You should see some droplets of water on the inside of the bag, indicating high humidity, but the bag should not be soaking wet. If the soil appears too wet, punch a few holes in the plastic bag or open it slightly to allow excess moisture to evaporate.

9. **After about two weeks, check for the presence of new roots by tugging very gently on the cuttings.** When you feel resistance the cuttings have developed roots and are ready for transplanting. If they haven't yet rooted, keep checking at regular intervals. Once you feel resistance, gently lift the cuttings using a spoon or other tool and transplant them into separate pots.

Bulbs

A bulb is a living "storehouse" that contains the embryonic stem, leaves, and flower of a plant. The bulb itself is a thickened underground stem that stores food for the growth of the plant. Bulbs have food reserves that enable them to grow and flower with no additional nutrients during the first year. Once a bulb flowers, the plant must take in nutrients and photosynthesize in order to develop reserves to flower again the following year.

Bulbs that you can easily grow or force in the classroom include crocuses, grape hyacinths, tulips, daffodils, and paperwhite narcissus.

How to Force Bulbs

1. **Purchase bulbs for forcing in the fall when hardy types are commonly available from garden centers and nursery catalogs.** If you can't plant them right away, store them in a cool (40° to 50°F), dry, dark spot. Because bulbs are living plants, you shouldn't leave them unplanted for long. Try to plant the bulbs by the end of October.

2. **Plant bulbs in 6-inch pots filled with moist soilless mix** (three bulbs per pot). Bury the bulbs to their tips, with pointed ends facing up. You don't need to add fertilizer.

3. **Put the pots in a place where the temperature will remain between 35° and 45°F,** such as an unheated garage, cold frame, or refrigerator, for a minimum of eight weeks. Since these bulbs are generally planted outdoors in fall for a spring bloom, this cold treatment will simulate the winter conditions necessary for them to form roots.

4. **Next, move containers inside and keep them in normal classroom light for two weeks,** then put them under your indoor garden lights or on a bright windowsill. The bulbs should bloom in two to four weeks. Once they begin blooming, move the plants from the bright light of the indoor garden to another bright, but cool, spot. This

Stimulating Rooting

A fifth-grade class, curious to find out which techniques might hasten the process of rooting in houseplant cuttings, set up an experiment to test various rooting methods. These methods included: dipping the cuttings in a commercial rooting hormone, providing bottom heat to the cuttings, feeding the cuttings with a fertilizer high in phosphorus, and even playing music for some cuttings! They compared the results of these trials with one another and with the control group and measured the total length of roots for each treatment after three weeks.

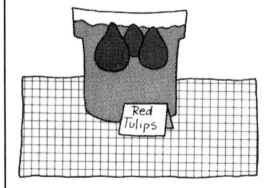

Red Tulips

Paperwhite narcissus are the only bulbs recommended here that **do not** require a chilling period. Plant as directed in step 2 at left and place the potted paperwhites in a window. They should set roots, grow leaves, and flower in just 6 weeks.

Growing Garlic

Garlic is another type of bulb that you can start indoors. Plant separate cloves with the flatter end down, 2 inches deep and 3 inches apart in soilless mix. Garlic doesn't like too much moisture, so allow the soil to dry thoroughly between waterings. It also isn't picky about lighting and will grow well in a GrowLab or on a windowsill.

Have children crush and smell some of the leaves and describe the characteristic smell. The bulbs form underground and are ready to harvest after the tops yellow, in three or four months. Use the garlic as an ingredient in your garden salad dressing or experiment with garlic juice as a pest remedy!

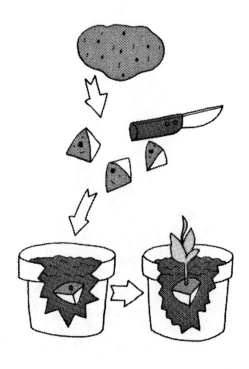

note:

Sweet potatoes produce beautiful vines. To start a sweet potato in water, leave it whole. Poke three toothpicks an even distance apart into the potato. Suspend the potato, purple-budded end up, one-third of the way into a jar of water.

will prevent blossoms from fading too quickly.

5. **If you want to save your bulbs,** remove the spent blooms, leave the foliage in place, and fertilize the plants every two weeks with plant food diluted according to the label instructions. During this time the bulbs produce and store food for next year's flowers. Rather than attempting to force these bulbs the following year, plant them outside. It may take two or more years before they'll produce another flush of blooms.

Tubers

A tuber is another type of underground stem that acts as a food storage organ. Tubers don't contain embryonic leaves and flowers as bulbs do but new plants grow from them. The most familiar example of a tuber is the potato. The surface of a potato has "eyes" that are actually buds. You can start new potato plants by planting pieces of tuber that contain eyes (explain to the children that this is exactly how farmers plant their potatoes.) Some grocery store potatoes have been treated with a chemical to discourage sprouting. To ensure that your potatoes sprout, start cuttings from several different potatoes or buy certified "seed potatoes" from a garden center.

Although you won't be able to grow potatoes to maturity in small containers indoors, students will be able to observe the early development of plants. (If you could grow potatoes to maturity indoors, you would find that the new tubers develop above the old ones and are attached by smaller stems to the main plant).

How to Grow a Potato Plant

You can start potatoes in growing mix, or sprout them in water so that you can view root development. The class can even design an experiment comparing the growth of potato plants in water versus in potting mix. In either case, cut potatoes so that there is at least one eye on every piece.

1. **To start potatoes in potting mix,** place each piece in a 6-inch pot so that the eyes are about 3/4 inch below the surface.

2. **To start potatoes in water,** you'll need toothpicks and a clear glass container. Poke three toothpicks an equal distance apart into a piece of potato, keeping the eyes on top. Set the potato, suspended by the toothpicks, over the mouth of the container. Add water to the container until it reaches the potato, but keep the eyes above the surface of the water.

Place pots or containers in the classroom light garden or on a window-sill. Remember, you won't be able to grow potatoes to maturity indoors in such small containers, but the class can observe early stages of development.

Grow a Mini-Orchard

Growing plants from leftover fruit seeds is an old classroom favorite. Although these plants will not mature into fruit-bearing trees, many do make nice houseplants. Fruit trees that grow in temperate climates, such as apples and pears, require a long chilling period before the seeds sprout, so tropical fruit seeds may be a better choice for a class project. Adventurous gardeners might like to experiment with both.

The following tropical fruit seeds will produce lovely plants for the classroom: avocado, orange, lemon, lime, and tangerine.

How to Grow an Avocado Plant

You can start an avocado seed in water (to view root development) or in soilless mix. Your students can design an experiment comparing these two growing methods.

1. **To start an avocado in water,** suspend the seed, pointed end up, two-thirds of the way into a jar of water, using toothpicks as supports. Place it under lights or on a windowsill and make sure water is always in contact with the seed. Germination will take about thirty days. Once the plant has a few leaves, transplant it into a pot of soilless mix.

2. **To start an avocado in potting mix,** fill a 4-inch pot halfway with moistened soilless mix. Put the seed, pointed end up, in the pot and fill the pot with mix to within 3/4 inch of the top of the seed. Place it under lights or on a windowsill and keep the mix evenly moist.

How to Grow a Citrus Plant

1. Soak seeds in water for 24 hours after removing them from fruit.

2. Fill a 4- or 6-inch pot with moist soilless mix and plant the seeds 1/2 inch deep.

3. Keep the soil evenly moist until seeds germinate, which should take about a month. Place the seedling in your light garden or on a sunny windowsill.

4. Pinch the top shoots back when the plants reach about 12 inches tall to encourage branching and compact growth.

How to Grow a Cool-Climate Fruit Plant

1. Fill 6-inch pots or flats with moist sand or peat moss. Plant apple or pear seeds about 1/2 inch deep.

2. Place the containers in an unheated garage or a refrigerator for three months to simulate winter temperatures. Then bring the containers indoors and place them in your light garden or in a sunny windowsill.

3. When seedlings have developed two sets of leaves, transplant them into permanent pots and grow as described above for citrus, pinching the top shoots to encourage branching and compact growth.

Forcing Branches

You can clip the branches of many spring-flowering shrubs and trees and bring them into the classroom to provide an early display of fragrant spring flowers. Timing is important when forcing branches. Cut them as described below, six weeks before they would normally bloom in your area.

Cut a 12- to 24-inch section of branch that has many plump flower buds (these are fatter than the leaf buds). Scrape the bottom three inches of the bark at the bottom of the branch with a knife or scissors and stand the branch in lukewarm water for a day. Next, move the cutting to a container of cool water and leave it in indirect light in the classroom. Each week, change the water and cut an inch off the stem. Mist the branches several times a week to stimulate spring rains and to keep the buds from dehydrating. Branches should start to blossom in about three weeks. Move the cuttings to a sunny location once the buds open, so they will develop good color.

Branches for Easy Forcing

pussy willow	flowering dogwood
azalea	forsythia
apple	

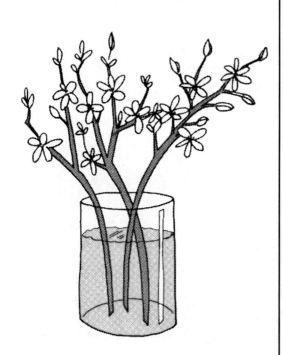

Growing Other Trees and Shrubs from Seeds

Collecting tree and shrub seeds from the wild to plant in the classroom garden allows students to explore another part of a plant's life cycle. Collect tree and shrub seeds as they mature, just before or after they drop in late summer or fall. If you can't work with these seeds within a day or two, store them in plastic bags in the refrigerator and, as soon as possible, perform the treatment described in How to Break Seed Dormancy (below).

To successfully germinate wild seeds, it's helpful for students to understand a bit about dormancy. Many tree and shrub seeds are naturally dispersed in the late summer or autumn. If they were to germinate at that point, the plant might have to survive unfavorable winter conditions. To avert this situation, many plants have developed control mechanisms that prevent the seeds from germinating until conditions are favorable.

One common form of dormancy results from a hard seed coat, which prevents the absorbtion of moisture required for germination. Another form of dormancy inhibits the development of the embryo until it has been subjected to cold winter temperatures. You and your students can create conditions in the indoor garden to break the dormancy of tree and shrub seeds collected from the outdoors.

How to Break Seed Dormancy

1. If the fruits have fleshy pulp that sticks to the seeds, wash the seeds before continuing.

2. If the seeds have hard coats (see the list below), use a hard object to scar or chip a small part of the seed coat away, or rub the seeds over a nail file or piece of sandpaper.

3. Place the seeds in moist peat moss, and put this mixture in a plastic bag.

4. Leave the plastic bag in a warm spot for three days. This will allow the seeds to take up water and swell.

5. Next, place the bag in a refrigerator for eight weeks.

6. Finally, remove the seeds and plant them as described in How to Grow a Cool-Climate Fruit Plant (page 81).

The following list identifies seeds that are easy to germinate indoors if you follow the appropriate steps. In nature, there is great variation between different trees and conditions under which their seeds germinate, so don't expect to have consistent results. Try different types of tree and shrub seedlings including those not listed here. You can also design experiments to see how different treatments affect seeds.

barberry	maple	*redbud
crab apple	oak	Russian olive
*honeysuckle	pine	sweet gum
*magnolia		

*These seeds have hard coats that require scarring.

Terrariums

A terrarium is a miniature garden/landscape grown inside a covered glass or plastic container. It is an excellent tool for learning about the water cycle. Since it is an enclosed environment, the original water evaporates, condenses against the container, precipitates to the soil, and then repeats the cycle. Some teachers have students create individual terrariums, while others prefer a collaborative class project.

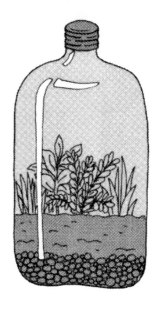

How to Build a Terrarium

1. **Find an appropriate container.** Glass jars, fish bowls and tanks, plastic shoeboxes, or the like can all make fine terrariums. Another option is to cut off the tops of large, clear, plastic soda bottles, leaving a container that is 8 inches tall.

2. **Clean the container well and cover the bottom with 1/2 inch of sand or gravel to improve drainage.** Then fill to one-third full with woodland soil, garden soil, or potting mix. The soil should be moist enough to cling together in balls when you squeeze it in your hand. If you can find it, add a few granules of the kind of charcoal sold in gardening stores (don't use barbecue charcoal unless you're sure that it doesn't contain additives to help with lighting). This will help filter out impurities and keep the soil in good condition in this closed system.

3. **Make small holes in the soil with your fingers to insert various plants.** Here are some suggestions:
   - rooted cuttings of ivy, begonia, coleus, spider plant, asparagus fern, peperomia
   - mosses, small flowering plants, tree seedlings, bits of bark, ferns, seeds (e.g., acorns) collected from outside
   - venus flytraps or other carnivorous plants from nurseries
   - mimosa seeds (these are available through some seed catalogs; they germinate quickly and look like miniature trees)

   Be creative and experiment with different seeds, plants, and objects to make a diverse mini-landscape. If something doesn't thrive or gets too big, replace it.

4. **Water the plants well and cover the container with the lid, a piece of plastic wrap, or glass.**

5. **Place the terrarium in your indoor garden or in a well-lighted classroom location.** Do not place it in direct sunlight or plants will scorch.

   You'll know that the terrarium contains the right amount of water if the sides and top get misty with water droplets when it's in bright light. If there is no moisture along the sides, you should add some water. If the sides are always very wet, there's too much water, and you should make holes in the lid or remove it for a few hours to let some water evaporate. If you achieve the perfect balance, you may not need to water again. Check the moisture periodically, to be sure.

6. **If you used soilless mix, you'll need to fertilize.** If you have used rich woodland soil, garden soil, or a potting mix with soil, you will not have to fertilize your terrariums. In fact, feeding would cause the plants to grow too large for their environment!

Appendix C

Reproducible Worksheets

KidsGardening.org and the Knox Parks Foundation grant permission and encourage teachers to copy the following worksheets for use with the GrowLab program:

– Plant Journal

– Plant Growth Chart

– A Trip Inside a Bean Seed

– The Life of a Bean Plant

– Flower Power

Keeping a Plant Journal

As you watch your plant grow, pay close attention to its progress. Notice how it changes in response to your care. Start a journal like the one below.

THINGS TO OBSERVE AND RECORD:

- How the seeds sprout
- When you water
- When you fertilize
- Changes in the plant as it grows
- Number of leaves
- Color and shape of leaves
- Number of flowers
- Height of the plant
- Movement of the plant
- Signs of pests and diseases
- Taste (if it's edible)
- Experimental treatments

To keep track of your plant's progress, start a diary like the one below.

Date and Time	Notes	Drawing
Sept. 9 9:30 am.	This morning my plant has no new leaves. It is nice and green. The plant is bending toward the sun. I am going to turn it around so the sun shines on the other side. The soil is a little dry. I will add ½ cup of water.	
Sept. 10 10:30 am.	My plant is starting to straighten up. Its 15 inches tall today. A pair of new leaves is starting to form. The soil is still wet so I won't water it today.	
Sept. 11 9:45 am.	My plant is bending toward the sun today!	

Name_____

Date and Time	Notes	Drawing

PLANT GROWTH CHART

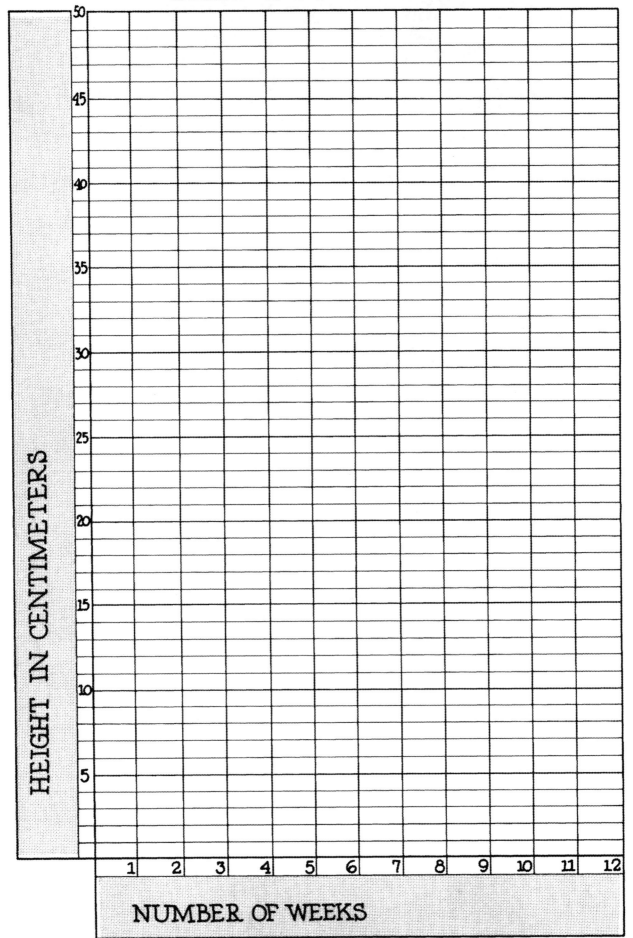

HEIGHT IN CENTIMETERS

NUMBER OF WEEKS

A TRIP INSIDE A BEAN SEED

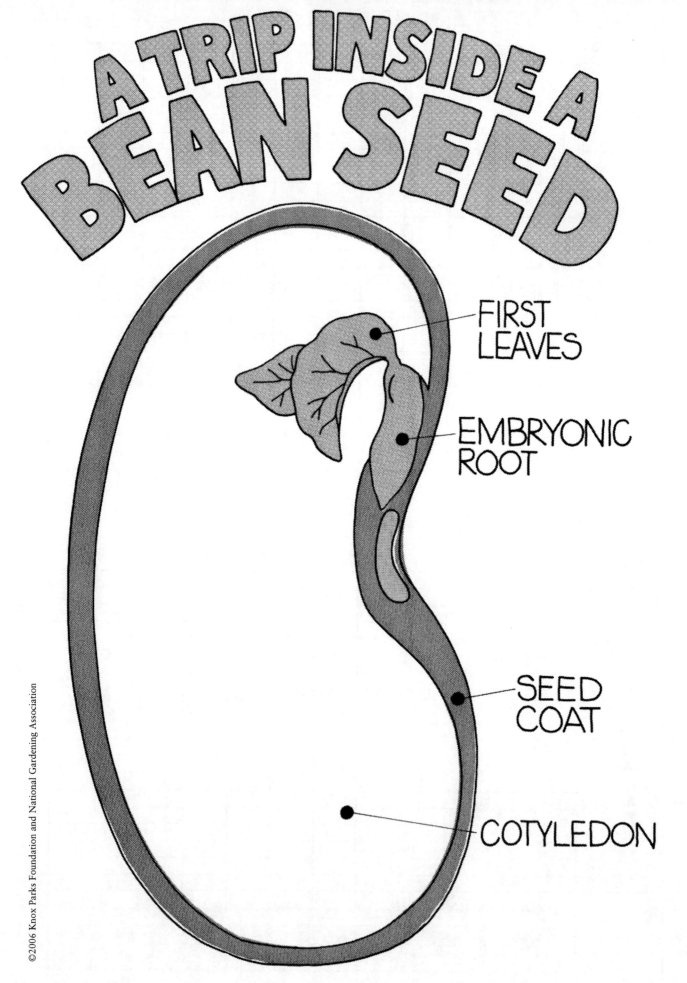

FIRST LEAVES

EMBRYONIC ROOT

SEED COAT

COTYLEDON

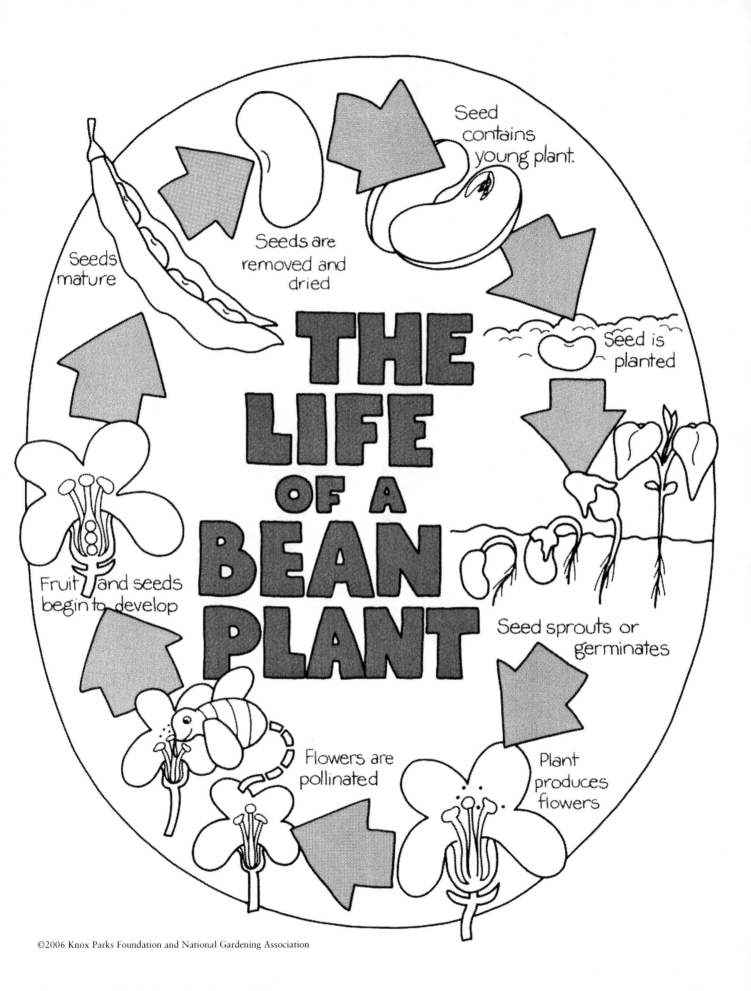

Seed contains young plant.

Seeds are removed and dried

Seeds mature

Seed is planted

THE LIFE OF A BEAN PLANT

Fruit and seeds begin to develop

Seed sprouts or germinates

Flowers are pollinated

Plant produces flowers

FLOWER POWER

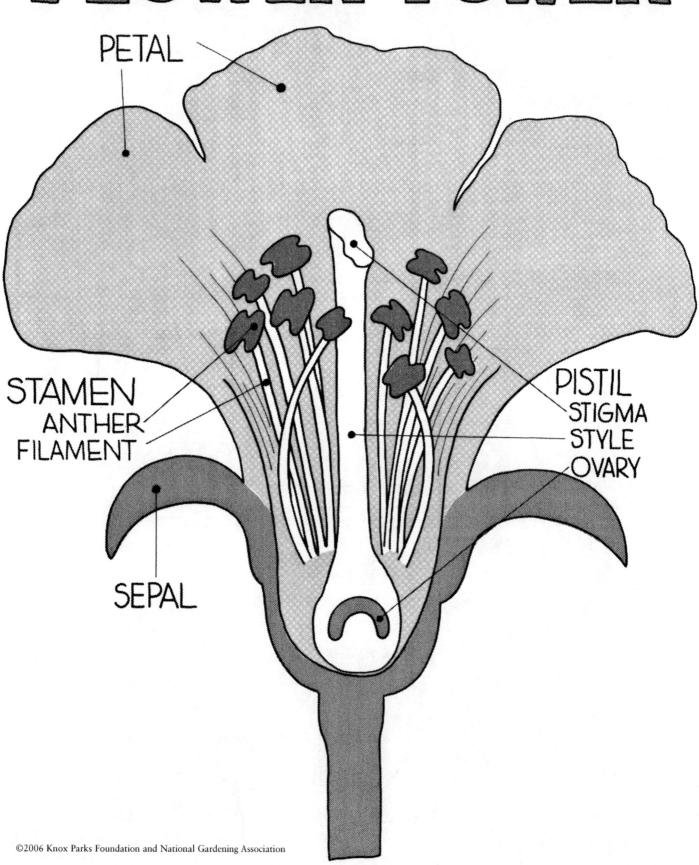

PETAL

STAMEN
ANTHER
FILAMENT

SEPAL

PISTIL
STIGMA
STYLE
OVARY

GrowLab: A Complete Guide to Gardening in the Classroom

Appendix D

Build-It-Yourself GrowLab

KidsGardening.org's build-it-yourself GrowLab construction plans have been reviewed by licensed electricians and expert carpenters. This unit is known to be safe, sturdy, and effective. The parts listed are easy to find and the procedures are straightforward. You may already have some of the materials and can save money by substituting your own or using recycled materials if they are in good condition.

These plans are divided into two sections:

1) Constructing the Wood Frame
2) Assembling Electrical Components

Before beginning this project, read through these instructions and study the diagrams in order to understand the scope of the project. This will help as you collect the proper tools and materials. Once you have the materials and tools you need, assembly of the GrowLab will take from seven to fifteen hours, depending on your level of expertise.

Constructing the Wooden Frame

You can purchase all of the materials for the wooden frame at a building supply store or lumber yard. The board dimensions and hardware are all standard sizes so that you can build the GrowLab with a minimum of tools. If you have access to a table saw, you can save money by cutting other pieces of new or recycled wood to size.

Using top-quality clear grade softwood (such pine or fir) for the frame will improve the finished appearance and make the assembly of your GrowLab easier. However, #2 grade lumber will cut costs considerably and is an acceptable substitution. If you choose the cheaper grade, try to get lengths that are straight and have few knots.

Frame Materials

- (5)   1"x 4"x 10' clear or # 2 grade lumber (actual dimensions 3/4"x 3 1/2"x 10')
- (2)   2"x 2"x 8' clear or #2 grade lumber (actual dimensions 1 1/2"x 1 1/2"x 8')
- (1)   48"x 24"x 3/8" CDX plywood (bought pre-cut or cut from a 4'x 8' sheet)
- (16)   3 x 1/4-20 slotted head bolts with nuts
- (32)   1/4" (inside diameter), 3/4" (outside diameter) flat washers
- (1 lb)   1 1/4" drywall screws
- (4)   3/4" drywall screws
- (1)   quart white exterior latex paint and brush
- (1)   small can wood filler, latex caulk, or Bondo (optional)
- (5)   sheets 100- or 120-grit sandpaper

Tools Required

– crosscut handsaw or electric circular saw
– carpenter's square
– tape measure
– electric drill
– 5/16" and 1/8" drill bits
– #1 Phillilps screwdriver bit or Phillips screwdriver
– adjustable wrench
– slotted screwdriver

Template Patterns (instructions on following page)

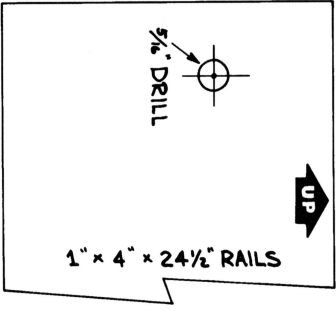

5/16" DRILL

UP

1" × 4" × 24½" RAILS

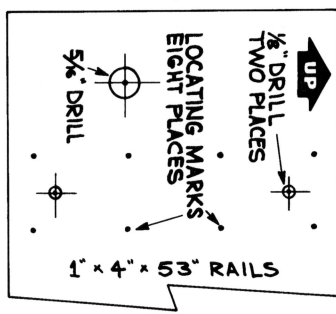

5/16" DRILL

LOCATING MARKS EIGHT PLACES

⅛" DRILL TWO PLACES

UP

1" × 4" × 53" RAILS

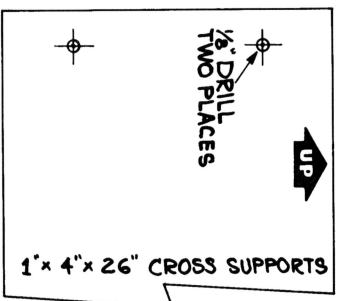

⅛" DRILL TWO PLACES

UP

1" × 4" × 26" CROSS SUPPORTS

Template Patterns Directions

Before beginning, make a photocopy of the three template patterns at left to preserve them for additional use. Follow these templates to mark drill holes and locating marks for your rails and cross supports after you've cut them to size according to the instructions on page 94.

Fig. 1A

1. Align template with left end of board. Use a sharp pencil to mark through the pattern to locate the drill hole.

2. Flip the pattern over so that printed side faces down; align on the right end of the board and mark.

Fig. 1B

1. Align template with left end of board. Use a sharp pencil to mark through the pattern for the three drill holes and the eight locating marks.

2. Flip the pattern over so that printed side faces down; align on the right end of board and mark.

Fig. 1C

1. Align template with left end of board. Use a sharp pencil to mark through the pattern to locate the drill holes.

2. Flip the pattern over so that printed side is face down; align on the right end of the board and mark.

Assembling the Frame

1. Cut List — Cut the lumber to the following sizes:

- (4)   1x4 rails @ 53"
- (4)   1x4 rails @ 24$1/2$"
- (6)   1x4 cross supports @ 26"
- (4)   2x2 posts @ 39"
- (1) $3/8$" plywood bottom @ 48"x 24" (cut if not pre-cut)

2. Bottom Frame Assembly

Step 1.   Following the instructions on template pattern figure 1A mark two 1"x 4"x 24$1/2$" rails for drill holes. Drill the marked spots with a $5/16$" drill bit.

Step 2.   Following the instructions on template pattern figure 1B mark two 1"x 4"x 53" rails for drill holes. Drill the marked spots with the bit sizes indicated: $5/16$" and $1/8$". Also mark the locating marks as shown on the template.

Step 3.   Assemble the bottom frame, as shown in figure 2, using two 53" rails and two 24$1/2$" rails. Fasten with eight 1$1/4$" drywall screws.

Step 4.   Following the instructions on template pattern figure 1C

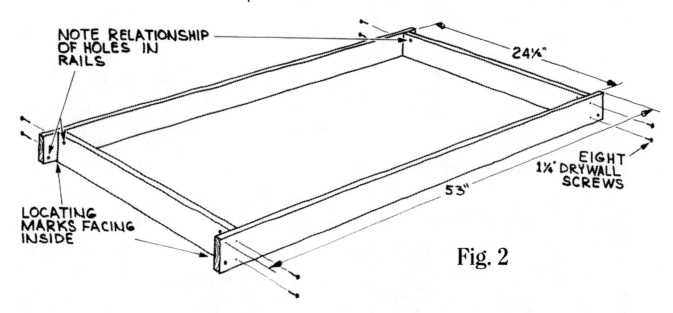

NOTE RELATIONSHIP OF HOLES IN RAILS

24¼"

53"

EIGHT 1¼" DRYWALL SCREWS

LOCATING MARKS FACING INSIDE

Fig. 2

mark four 1"x 4"x 26" cross supports for drill holes. Drill the marked spots using a $1/8$" drill bit.

Step 5.   Attach the four 26" cross supports to the bottom frame assembly using sixteen 1$1/4$" drywall screws as shown in figure 3.

Step 6.   Flip the bottom frame assembly over and insert and fasten the plywood bottom to the cross supports using four $3/4$" drywall screws as show in figure 4.

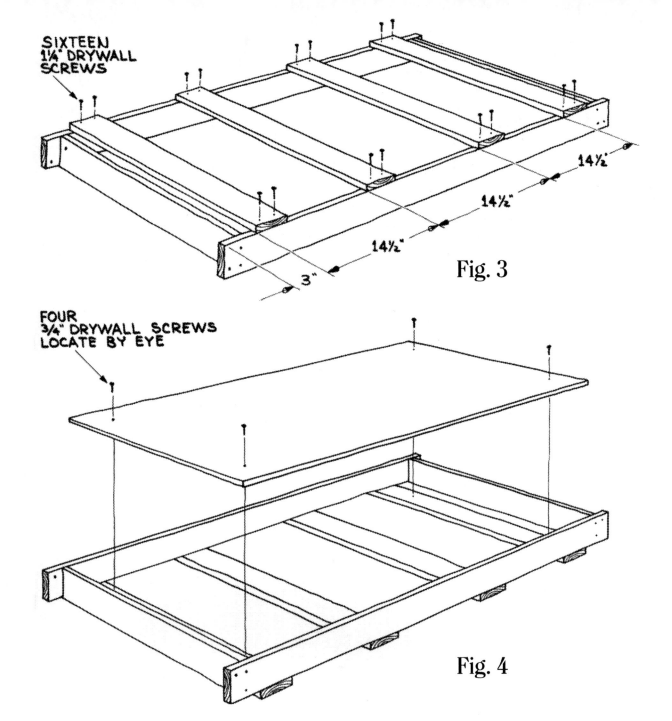

SIXTEEN
1¼" DRYWALL
SCREWS

3"

14½"

14½"

14½"

14½"

Fig. 3

FOUR
¾" DRYWALL SCREWS
LOCATE BY EYE

Fig. 4

3. Top Frame Assembly

Step 1. Follow Bottom Frame Assembly Steps 1 and 2 to mark and drill remaining rails using template patterns 1A and 1B.

Step 2. Assemble the top frame (same as bottom frame, as shown in figure 2) using two 53" rails and two 24 1/2" rails, and fasten with eight 1 1/4" drywall screws.

4. Attaching Top Frame to Bottom Frame

Step 1. Set a 2"x 2"x 39" post in position against the bottom frame as shown in figure 5. Through the two predrilled holes in the frame corner rails, mark the post for drill holes with a pencil or appropriate size punch.

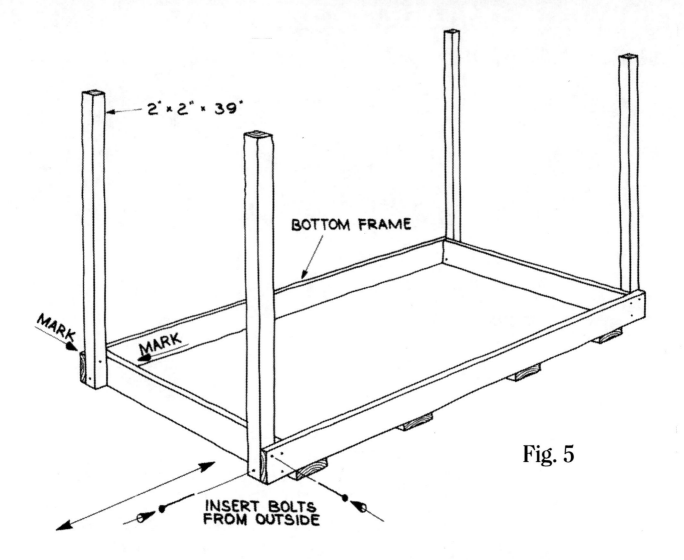

2" x 2" x 39"

BOTTOM FRAME

MARK

MARK

Fig. 5

INSERT BOLTS
FROM OUTSIDE

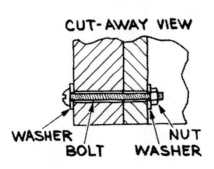

CUT-AWAY VIEW

WASHER   NUT
    BOLT   WASHER

Step 2. Remove post and drill holes using a ⁵/₁₆" bit.

Step 3. Attach the post to the bottom frame as shown in figure 5 (cut-away view) using one 3" bolt, two washers and one nut. Do not fully tighten the nut. Repeat steps 1 through 3 for the other three posts and corners.

Step 4. Place the top frame assembly on a flat work surface. Flip the bottom frame assembly with posts over and align it with top frame as show in figure 6 (page 97). Use a pencil to mark one post for drill holes through the two pre-drilled holes in the frame corners, as in Step 1. Mark the three remaining posts.

Step 5. Remove bottom frame assembly with four posts and place upright. Drill marked holes in posts using a ⁵/₁₆" bit.

Step 6. Place bottom frame assembly with posts back into top frame assembly as in Step 4 and attach one post to the top frame assembly using one 3" bolt, two washers, and a nut as in Step 3 (figure 5). Repeat for other posts.

Step 7. Using an adjustable wrench, tighten all sixteen nuts on bottom and top assembly and flip unit upright.

GrowLab: A Complete Guide to Gardening in the Classroom

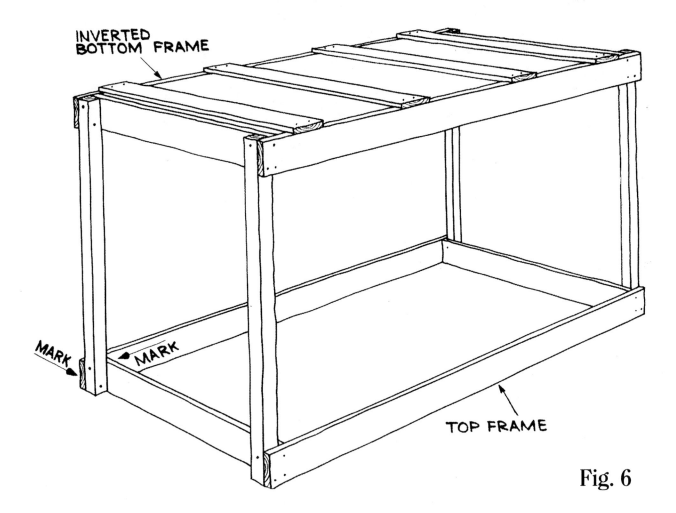

Fig. 6

5. Mounting Top Light Supports

Step 1. Following instructions in template pattern figure 1C, mark two 1"x 4"x 26" cross supports for drill holes. Drill the marked spots with a 1/8" drill bit.

Step 2. Measure the distance between the two existing holes on fluorescent fixture used for hanging the fixture, as shown in figure 7.

Fig. 7

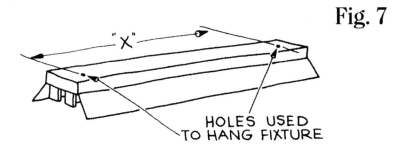

HOLES USED TO HANG FIXTURE

Step 3. Use this dimension as the approximate center-to-center measurement to locate the two remaining 26" cross supports on top of the top frame, as shown in figure 7A. Fasten with eight 1 1/4" drywall screws.

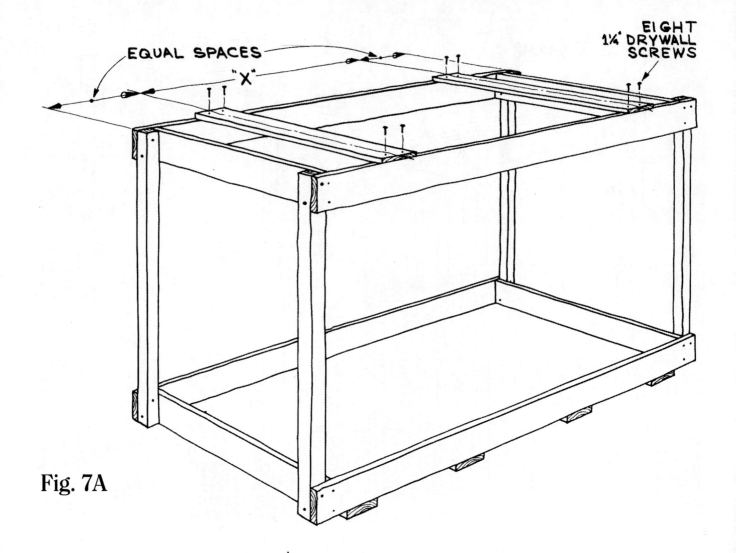

EQUAL SPACES

"X"

EIGHT 1¼" DRYWALL SCREWS

Fig. 7A

6. Finishing the Frame

Step 1.   Fill all holes and defects with wood putty; sand rough spots.

Step 2.   Paint using two coats of white exterior latex paint.

Assembling Electrical Components

Tools Required

– sharp knife
– slotted screwdriver
– Phillips screwdriver or electric drill with #1 Phillips bit
– heavy-duty wire cutter
– wire stripper
– needle-nose pliers

Electrical Materials

(3) UL-listed 48" two-tube fluorescent light fixtures; choose fixtures you can open to access the ballast and rewire the cord (see important information on page 100 regarding purchasing fixtures)

The following materials list and instructions assume you will be rewiring 3 light fixtures.

(1) UL-listed residential grade ground fault circuit interrupter receptacle (GFCI) and cover plate

(20) feet of 16/3 copper electrical cord (you can use heavier wire, #14 or #12, but do not use smaller wire, which has a gauge number higher than 16)

(4) three-prong electric plug and cap

(1) metal 2"x 4" surface-mounted electrical outlet box

(1) UL-listed, surface-mounted, multi-outlet receptacle strip (4-6 outlets) with grounded plug cord

(4) 1/2" Romex connector collar

(9) small wire nuts (note: wire nuts may come with light fixtures)

(4) 3/4" drywall screws

(6) eye hooks

(12) s-hooks (note: 2 s-hooks may come with each light fixture)

(18) feet of #3 chain

(1) 20' self-regulating heating cable (optional)

(1) 28"x 54" sheet of 6 mil plastic

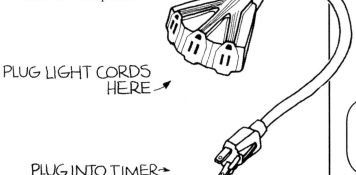

PLUG LIGHT CORDS HERE ➔

PLUG INTO TIMER ➔

note:

You won't need to rewire light fixtures if you can find UL-listed light fixtures with an extra-long power cord (36" from the end of the fixture or 60" from the center of the fixture). However, it is difficult to find such fixtures. This extra length is required to allow for height adjustment of light fixtures. If you have these fixtures you may eliminate three Romex connectors, ten feet of 16/3 copper electrical cable, three electric plugs (three prong), and all wire nuts from your materials list.

You can also avoid wiring fixtures if you can locate the type of 2-foot, 12-gauge, grounded, UL-listed, three-outlet adapter illustrated below. In this case, you can use light fixtures with short cords and may eliminate the materials described above as well as the multi-outlet receptacle and Steps 1 through 5 under Installing Lights.

Instead of rewiring light fixtures, plug the short cords on your fixtures directly into the three-outlet adapter. Plug the other end of the adapter plug directly into your grounded timer.

Use only receptacles, plugs, and electrical devices that are grounded.

Purchasing Electrical Supplies

You can purchase most electrical supplies at well-stocked lumber and building, hardware, or department stores. Industrial-grade light fixtures and grounded timers can be purchased at electrical supply stores.

Fluorescent Fixtures — You may use various types of fluorescent light fixtures in a GrowLab. Shop lights, which cost between $15 and $30, are the type you will probably find at discount or hardware stores. They have metal side reflectors that direct light onto plants and help prevent tube breakage. Shop lights are often built with a low-quality ballast, which may decrease the life expectancy of the fixture.

Higher-grade light fixtures with heavy-duty ballasts are available at electrical supply stores for $40 to $50. The ballasts on these higher-grade fixtures last longer and make less noise than shop lights. Look for fixtures with metal side reflectors and at least 4 inches between bulbs to provide better light distribution to plants.

LED Fixtures — There are also a number of LED light fixtures available for your GrowLab. Although, usually a bit more expensive, they have the added benefits of using less electricity, lasting five times longer than fluorescent bulbs, producing less heat, along with being mercury free and shatter resistant. Most hardware stores will offer full-spectrum LED lights and equipment in the same location as fluorescent lighting with similar selections in frames. You can also find LED lights specifically designed for plant growth through specialty retailers such as Gardener's Supply Company.

Heating Cable — If your GrowLab will reside in a room that seems too cool to promote good plant growth (see page 47), you can install a heating cable beneath the base material. (See lighting and electrical wiring assembly procedures for information on installing your heating cable.)

A self-regulating, three-watt heating cable requires no thermostat. This type of heating cable can be purchased at hardware stores by the foot, along with a do-it-yourself end cap and plug.

Heating cables with built-in thermostats are available at many garden centers. These are often referred to as soil heating cables. Be careful when installing and using this type of cable, as it can burn out if misused.

Ground-Fault Circuit Interrupter — A ground-fault circuit interrupter (GFCI) protects you against hazardous electrical shock that may be caused if your body becomes a path through which electricity travels to reach ground. If there is a short circuit, the GFCI will cut off quickly enough to avoid electrical injury.

Ground faults should be tested every three months by pushing the "test" button. The test creates an internal short circuit to check if the system works. If functioning properly, the "reset" button will pop out. Push the reset button back to its normal position. If it does not move, the ground-fault circuit interrupter is not functioning and should be replaced.

Wiring Electrical Controls

1. Mounting Electrical Outlet Boxes

Step 1.   Fasten the 2"x 4" electrical box and the multi-outlet strip receptacle to the left top rail, using four ³/4" dry-wall screws, as shown in figure 8.

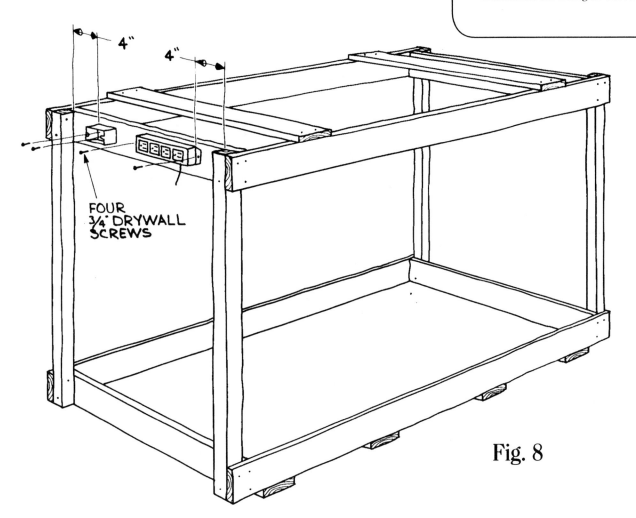

FOUR ³/4" DRYWALL SCREWS

Fig. 8

2. Wiring Power Supply (power cable, plug, GFCI)

Step 1.   Cut one piece of 16/3 electrical cable 10' long. Use a knife to remove 1" of outer insulation from one end — be careful not to cut the insulation of the three inner wires. Use the wire strippers to remove ¹/2" of insulation from each of the three inner wires, as shown in figure 9.

Step 2.   Attach each of the three inner wires to the appropriate screw of the three-prong plug, as shown in figure 9. Tighten the three internal screws, the two strain relief screws, and reattach the fiber cover.

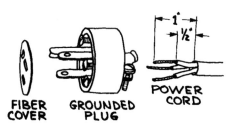

FIBER COVER   GROUNDED PLUG   POWER CORD

WHITE WIRE TO SILVER SCREW
BLACK WIRE TO BRONZE SCREW
GREEN WIRE TO GREEN SCREW

Fig. 9

Fig. 10

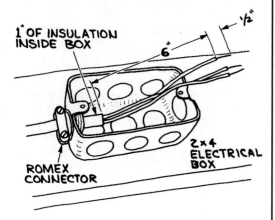

1" OF INSULATION
INSIDE BOX

6"

1/2"

ROMEX
CONNECTOR

2 x 4
ELECTRICAL
BOX

Step 3. From the opposite end of the 10' piece of cable remove 4" of outer insulation and 1/2" of insulation from the ends of the three inner wires, as shown in figure 10, following the same procedures as Step 1.

Step 4. Remove a circular "knock-out" from the electrical box and install a Romex connector in the box as shown in figure 10. Insert stripped end of the cable through the connector into the box so that 1" of unstripped cable is inside the box as shown in figure 10. Tighten the two screws on the Romex connector.

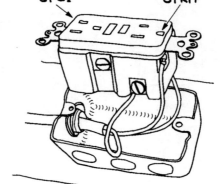

GROUND LUG
TOWARDS
RECEPTACLE
STRIP

GFCI

Fig. 11

MAKE ALL CONNECTIONS TO
"LINE" SIDE OF GFCI.
WHITE WIRE TO "WHITE" SCREW
BLACK WIRE TO "HOT" SCREW
GREEN WIRE TO "GREEN" SCREW

note:

Always use the stripping guides on the GFCI receptacles for stripping back to bare wire when attaching wire to the GFCI receptacle. Also, whenever stripping wire to be connected by wire nuts, be sure that no bare wire is exposed below the end of the wire nut.

Step 5. Install the ground fault circuit interrupter as shown in figure 11, following the wiring and orientation directions. Fasten the GFCI to the electrical box and attach cover.

Step 6. Plug the timer into the GFCI and the cable from the multi-outlet receptacle strip into the timer as shown in figure 12.

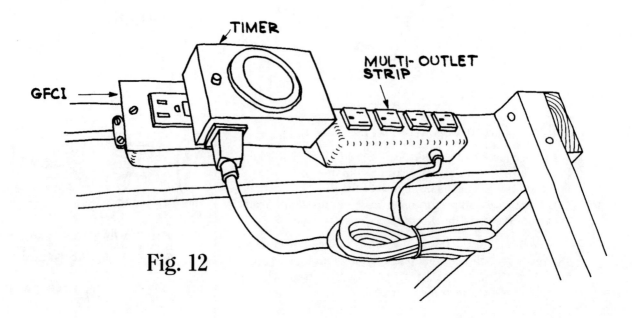

TIMER

MULTI-OUTLET
STRIP

GFCI

Fig. 12

GrowLab: A Complete Guide to Gardening in the Classroom

Installing Lights

1. Wiring Light Fixtures

If you must add longer cords to your fixtures, repeat Steps 1 through 5 for each fixture.

Step 1. Open up the light fixture by removing the retaining hardware or following manufacturer's directions. If there is an existing cord, follow where the existing cord enters the fixture until the inner wires terminate at wire nuts. Remove the wire nuts and the cord. Make a note of where all wires are connected.

Step 2. Cut a 40" length of 16/3 cable and install a three-prong plug following same directions as in Wiring Power Supply, Steps 1 and 2 (see figure 9).

Step 3. From the opposite end of the cable, remove 4"-6" of outer insulation and 1/2" of insulation from the ends of the three inner wires, as in Wiring Power Supply, Step 3.

Step 4. Feed cable cord through hole in the end of the fixture until wire ends meet ballast connections. Be sure to leave at least 1" of unstripped cable inserted into fixture. Place one Romex connector where the cable enters the fixture and secure it tightly as in figure 13.

Step 5. Attach the new cord to the fixture, making sure to connect the new inner wires to the appropriate wires in the fixture, as shown in figure 13. Use wire nuts to make all connections. Reattach cover to light fixture.

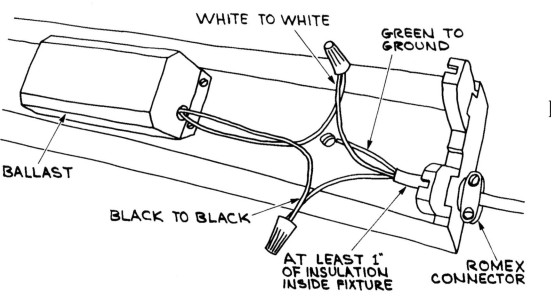

WHITE TO WHITE

GREEN TO GROUND

Fig. 13

BALLAST

BLACK TO BLACK

AT LEAST 1" OF INSULATION INSIDE FIXTURE

ROMEX CONNECTOR

OTHER WIRING OMITTED FOR CLARITY

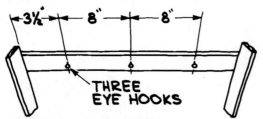

← 3½" → ← 8" → ← 8" →

THREE
EYE HOOKS

VIEW OF TWO TOP
CROSS SUPPORTS
FROM UNDERNEATH

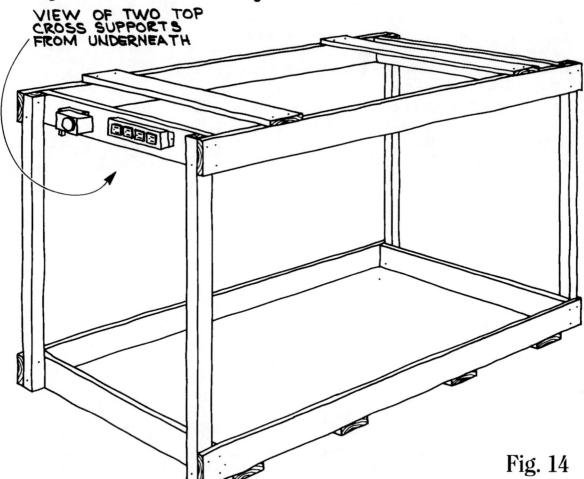

Fig. 14

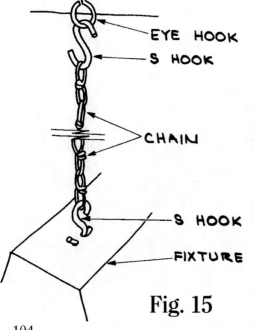

EYE HOOK

S HOOK

CHAIN

S HOOK

FIXTURE

Fig. 15

2. Mounting the Lights

Step 1.   Screw six eye hooks into the two top cross supports of the wood frame, following the directions shown in figure 14.

Step 2.   Cut six lengths of chain 36" long.

Step 3.   Using four S-hooks and two lengths of chain, hang each light as shown in figure 15. Close the bottom S-hooks on the light fixtures with pliers. Install fluorescent tubes with tube guards. Plug each light into the receptacle strip.

GrowLab: A Complete Guide to Gardening in the Classroom

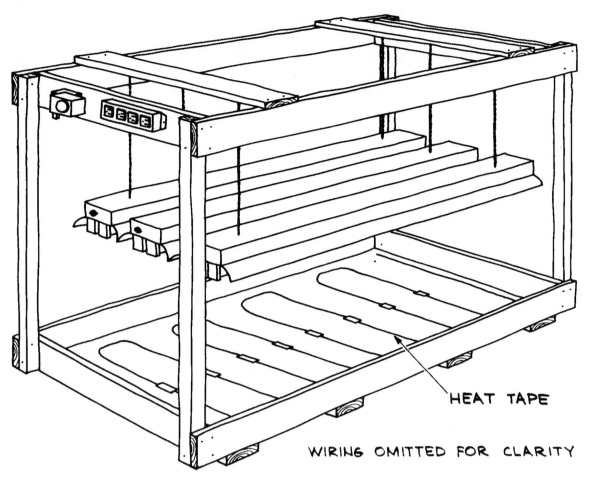

Fig. 16

HEAT TAPE

WIRING OMITTED FOR CLARITY

3. Installing a Heating Cable (Optional)

Step 1.   If you use a self-regulating cable, follow directions that come with heating cable for connecting the end cap and plug.

Step 2.   Unless you have a plastic tray, lay a 28"x 54" plastic sheet in the base of the GrowLab frame with edges at the same level as the top of the rails.

Step 3.   Lay the heating cable over the plastic in the bottom of the unit, as illustrated in figure 16, making sure not to cross the cable back over itself.

Step 4.   Tape cable in place using electrical or duct tape. (During operation, the cable will be covered with 2" of moist sand/perlite, or with capillary matting.)

Step 5.   Plug the heating cable directly into the ground fault receptacle. Do not plug heating cable into multi-outlet strip or timer as that will turn cable on and off.

Shopping List for a Build-It-Yourself GrowLab

Make a photocopy of the chart below, then use the chart to shop around for supplies, since costs can vary tremendously. Many teachers have cut assembly costs considerably by using recycled materials.

Materials Cost Comparison Grid

Source 1: _____

Source 2: _____

Source 3: _____

Material	Source 1 Price ($)	Source 2 Price ($)	Source 3 Price ($)
lumber (clear grade)			
hardware for frame			
paint and brush			
wood filler			
sandpaper			
3 light figures (shop lights)			
grounded timer			
multi-outlet strip			
ground-fault circuit interrupter and outlet box			
electrical cord			
three-prong plugs			
6 cool white tubes			
electrical hardware			
chains and hooks			
Total	$	$	$

KidsGardening

As a national 501(c)(3) nonprofit organization, KidsGardening offers educators, garden volunteers and parents support to provide the children in their lives with learning experiences that begin in the garden and stay with them the rest of their lives — resulting in improved academics, better eating habits, greater environmental stewardship, and ultimately healthier, more secure and engaged communities.

Our Mission

To empower every generation to lead healthier lives, build stronger communities, and encourage environmental stewardship through educational gardening programs.

We offer a variety of resources to "Help Young Minds Grow" including:

Kidsgardening.org

Our website strives to be an interactive hub where teachers, parents and others who garden with kids find inspiration, advice, and opportunities for growth. Featuring an extensive collection of lesson plans and hands-on activities, you'll also find comprehensive horticultural guides and information on how to develop successful youth gardening educational programs.

Grants and Awards

Looking for ways to expand your school or organization's garden? Since 1982, KidsGardening has enriched the lives of an estimated 1.5 million youth participants across America and around the world. Over 10,000 awards, totaling $4.4 million, have been distributed to install or enhance youth garden programs.

Free eNewsletter

Wondering what's new in the world of kids' gardening? Check out KidsGarden News, our monthly email newsletter, which highlights thematic activities and engaging lesson plans. You will also find activities that are great for home gardens too. Features up-to-date funding and grant opportunities along with upcoming events. Subscribe today!

Growing Ideas Blog

Searching for garden inspiration? With a new post weekly direct from our staffers, the Growing Ideas Blog brings you timely gardening news, growing tips, learning activities, and ideas for developing your garden. See what we are excited about and join the conversation.